Of all the changes that COVID-19 has demanded, the rise of remote working is among the most likely to stick long term. This excellent book gives an accessible yet thoroughly research-based account of the key issues – from the historical development of remote working, to the forms it takes (including hybrid working) and the implications for people management and quality of working life.

—Jonny Gifford, *Senior Advisor for Organisational Behaviour, Chartered Institute of Personnel and Development.*

The author's 25 years of seminal scholarship on homeworking gives credibility and authority to his reflections on the nature of remote working in the post-pandemic era. This is a concise and essential book for researchers, employers and remote-working employees.

—Professor Brendan Burchell, *Professor of Sociology, University of Cambridge.*

This book offers an excellent resource for those researching or interested in learning more about remote and hybrid working. With relevance to academics, practitioners, policy-makers and students, this book provides important insights into historical and current trends, impacts for employees and employers, and the potential future of work. In the spirit of hybrid working don't just buy one copy of this book, buy two, one for when you are working at the office and one for when you are working at home!

—Dr Dan Wheatley, *Reader in Business and Labour Economics, University of Birmingham.*

This is an excellent exposition of the history, present and future of remote working based on robust research evidence. A must read for anyone interested in how the changing location of work affects our lives.

—Professor Ying Zhou, *Professor of Human Resource Management, University of Surrey.*

Remote Working

The coronavirus pandemic forced work back into the home on a massive scale. The long-held belief that work and home are separate spheres of economic life was turned on its head overnight.

Many employees were new to this way of working and many employers had to manage a disparate workforce for the first time. This book reviews what impact this shift had on the lives of millions of employees, the organisations which employ them, and the societies in which they live. It also looks to a future in which more work is carried out remotely – at home, in the local café, restaurant, or bar, or while moving from place to place. The book syntheses the existing evidence in an accessible and easy-to-read way.

It will appeal to all those who want a quick and concise introduction to the major themes associated with remote and hybrid working. This includes teachers, lecturers, students, academics, and policymakers as well as those who have experienced the challenges and benefits of homeworking first-hand.

Alan Felstead is Research Professor at the School of Social Sciences, Cardiff University, UK.

State of the Art in Business Research
Series Editor: Geoffrey Wood

Recent advances in theory, methods and applied knowledge (alongside structural changes in the global economic ecosystem) have presented researchers with challenges in seeking to stay abreast of their fields and navigate new scholarly terrains.

State of the Art in Business Research presents shortform books which provide an expert map to guide readers through new and rapidly evolving areas of research. Each title will provide an overview of the area, a guide to the key literature and theories and time-saving summaries of how theory interacts with practice.

As a collection, these books provide a library of theoretical and conceptual insights, and exposure to novel research tools and applied knowledge, that aid and facilitate in defining the state of the art, as a foundation stone for a new generation of research.

Gossip, Organization and Work
A Research Overview
Kathryn Waddington

Remote Working
A Research Overview
Alan Felstead

Business History
A Research Overview
John F. Wilson, Ian G. Jones, Steven Toms, Anna Tilba, Emily Buchnea and Nicholas Wong

For more information about this series, please visit: www.routledge.com/State-of-the-Art-in-Business-Research/book-series/START

Remote Working

A Research Overview

Alan Felstead

R Routledge
Taylor & Francis Group

LONDON AND NEW YORK

First published 2022
by Routledge
4 Park Square, Milton Park, Abingdon, Oxon OX14 4RN

and by Routledge
605 Third Avenue, New York, NY 10158

Routledge is an imprint of the Taylor & Francis Group, an informa business

British Library Cataloguing-in-Publication Data
A catalogue record for this book is available from the British Library

Library of Congress Cataloging-in-Publication Data
Names: Felstead, Alan, 1963– author.
Title: Remote working: a research overview/Alan Felstead.
Description: Milton Park, Abingdon, Oxon; New York, NY: Routledge, 2022. |
  Series: State of the art in business research | Includes bibliographical references and index.
Identifiers: LCCN 2021048656 (print) | LCCN 2021048657 (ebook) | ISBN
  9781032160986 (hardback) | ISBN 9781032161037 (paperback) | ISBN
  9781003247050 (ebook)
Subjects: LCSH: Telecommuting. | COVID-19 Pandemic, 2020–
Classification: LCC HD2336.3 .F45 2022 (print) | LCC HD2336.3 (ebook) |
  DDC 658.3/123 – dc23/eng/20211012
LC record available at https://lccn.loc.gov/2021048656
LC ebook record available at https://lccn.loc.gov/2021048657

ISBN: 978-1-032-16098-6 (hbk)
ISBN: 978-1-032-16103-7 (pbk)
ISBN: 978-1-003-24705-0 (ebk)

DOI: 10.4324/9781003247050

Typeset in Times New Roman
by Apex CoVantage, LLC

This book is dedicated to Christine Felstead, my Mum, who died on 22 July 2021, while this book was being written.

Contents

List of Figures

List of Tables

Acknowledgements

Studying the location of work has been a research interest of mine ever since Nick Jewson and I secured a government-sponsored research project to study industrial homeworkers. That was back in 1993. The project was funded by what was then the Employment Department. It involved carrying out one of the largest surveys of industrial homeworkers ever conducted in Britain. Several other research projects followed: first, a study of white-collar homeworkers and then a second study of how workers used places other than their homes and employers' premises – such as trains, cars, and hotels – to carry out their work. These Economic and Social Research Council (ESRC) projects involved working with Nick Jewson, who inspired, and continues to inspire, my thinking today. Periodically, I have updated and extended this work as more data and evidence have become available. In the pursuit of these endeavours, I have had the pleasure of working with John Goodwin, Annie Phizacklea, Sally Walters, and Golo Henseke. More recently, the growth of homeworking prompted by the pandemic peeked my interest in the subject once again. This has led to collaborative work with Darja Reuschke. I would like to thank all of these colleagues for the insights that joint working has provided. I would also like to acknowledge that some of the figures and tables in this book were produced using particular data sets. These include the Labour Force Survey, the Understanding Society Covid-19 Study, the Skills and Employment Survey, and Eurofound's Living, Working and Covid-19 Survey. However, the data owners do not bear any responsibility for the interpretation of the data or the ideas and arguments presented in this book. Lorraine Felstead deserves a special mention for proofreading the manuscript, pointing out how my grammar and/ or sentence construction could be improved, and putting up with me during the three months in the summer of 2021 when the book was written. Finally, I acknowledge all of the authors cited in this book for their outstanding and timely research since without them there would be little to say.

Alan Felstead
September 2021

List of Abbreviations

ACAS	Advisory, Conciliation and Arbitration Service
ASHE	Annual Survey of Hours and Earnings
ATUS	American Time Use Survey
BEIS	Department for Business, Energy and Industrial Strategy
BICS	Business Insights and Conditions Survey
BLS	US Bureau of Labor Statistics
CBI	Confederation of British Industry
CEO	Chief Executive Officer
CIPD	Chartered Institute of Personnel and Development
DSE	Display Screen Equipment
ESRC	Economic and Social Research Council
EU	European Union
EWCS	European Working Conditions Survey
HSE	Health and Safety Executive
ICT	Information and Communications Technology
ILO	International Labour Organisation
IoD	Institute of Directors
IZ	Intermediate Zone
LFS	Labour Force Survey
LOC	Leicester Outwork Campaign
MES	Management and Expectations Survey
MOPS	Management and Organisational Practices Survey
MSOA	Middle Layer Super Output Area
NGH	National Group on Homeworking
OECD	Organisation for Economic Co-operation and Development
ONS	Office for National Statistics
SES	Skills and Employment Survey
TUC	Trades Union Congress
WERS	Workplace Employment Relations Survey

About the Author

Alan Felstead is Research Professor at the School of Social Sciences, Cardiff University. He has a long-standing interest in the changing location of work which began in the mid-1990s. He has produced hundreds of publications on this and other labour market issues. In addition, he has given oral and written evidence to the Department of Work and Pensions Select Committee, the House of Lords Covid-19 Committee, and the Scottish and Welsh Parliaments. In 2018–2019, he sat on the Welsh Government's Fair Work Commission and was then seconded to Welsh Government on a part-time basis in 2019–2020. He is also a member of the ESRC-supported Wales Institute of Social and Economic Research and Data (WISERD), and a Visiting Professor at the Centre for Research on Learning and Life Chances (LLAKES), UCL Institute of Education.

1 Setting the Scene

'Never let a good crisis go to waste', Winston Churchill, sometime in the mid-1940s.

1.1 Introduction

A prolonged period of being asked – sometimes instructed – to work at home has meant that many more of us have experienced working remotely, that is, outside the premises of the employer. For that reason, the book is titled *Remote Working: A Research Overview*. However, as will become clear, the coronavirus pandemic has raised fundamental questions about where we work and why, and whether it represents a pivotal moment from which there is no turning back. The location of work has received enormous attention as governments around the world have placed unprecedented restrictions on what their citizens can and cannot do, and where they are allowed to go.

In a bid to limit the spread of the coronavirus, many national governments curbed the ability of citizens to meet others and to move freely within and across national boundaries. Directly and indirectly this changed the ways in which people work and where they do so. Given that large numbers of people have traditionally gathered in workplaces and used public transport to move from A to B, the first response of governments was to limit physical interaction in offices, factories, and shops as well as on trains and buses. Another tactic was to promote working at home, hence limiting large workplace gatherings and removing one of the major reasons for travel. Out of 51 countries surveyed by the Organisation for Economic Co-operation and Development (OECD) in mid-2020, all but 5 were either encouraging or instructing segments of their population to work at home (OECD, 2020). At around the same time, 59 countries were mandating their directly employed, non-public-facing staff to work at home (ILO, 2020). A more drastic response was to impose national and/or regional lockdowns which further encouraged the employed population to work at home if possible.

DOI: 10.4324/9781003247050-1

In the face of these restrictions, homeworking rocketed. Across Europe as a whole, 37% of the working population reported working at home in April 2020 because of the pandemic with homeworking rates close to 60% in Finland and above 50% in Luxembourg, the Netherlands, Belgium, and Denmark (Eurofound, 2020). In the US, around a third (35%) of the workforce in April 2020 reported ditching the daily commute and working at home instead (Brynjolfsson *et al.*, 2020). Employers, too, changed their behaviour. In line with government advice, many high-profile companies – such as Google, Twitter, Apple, Microsoft, Amazon, and JP Morgan – closed their offices and ordered their staff to work at home (*BBC News*, 11 March 2020; *Financial Times*, 11 January 2021a).

Interest in the shift of work away from traditional workplaces and into the home can also be seen in the newspaper column inches, internet blogs, and TV and radio reports devoted to the subject. For example, newspaper articles in the UK on working from home – published in national broadsheets and tabloids, and in regional and local news outlets – rose from around 150 per month before the outbreak of Covid-19 to a monthly peak of almost 6,000 in March 2020. Working from home remained a hot topic for the remainder of the year with an average of 3,600 newspaper articles appearing on the subject every month. Its popularity continued into 2021 with thousands of column inches devoted to the issues surrounding working from home (see Figure 1.1). As the following headlines demonstrate, these articles have succinctly covered many of the issues addressed in this book. They have:

- mapped the growth of homeworking – 'Where were the homeworking hotspots in 2020?' (*London Standard*, 17 May 2021);
- identified who is thriving and who is struggling to cope – 'Homeworking isn't working, at least for the young' (*The Independent*, 24 March 2021);
- listed the benefits that employers gain from these 'new' ways of working – 'Offices: homeworking will save employers billions' (*Financial Times*, 8 April 2021b);
- noted the relatively benign impact on business performance – 'Home workers get more done during pandemic, study finds' (*The Daily Telegraph*, 1 April 2021);
- outlined the dangers of keeping the world of work and home separate – 'Homeworking sounds good – until your job takes over your life' (*The Guardian*, 7 March 2021);
- highlighted how employees may lose out – 'Homeworking is depriving me of juicy gossip' (*Financial Times*, 13 July 2020a);
- identified the pluses for society – 'Gentler, greener, quieter: welcome to the city of the future' (*The Daily Telegraph*, 1 December 2020) – as well as the minuses – 'Empty offices are killing town centres' (*Daily Mail*, 10 July 2020);

- provided a sober account of the scale of the long-term change – 'Death of the office exaggerated despite the homeworking boom' (*Financial Times*, 1 July 2020b); and
- highlighted the increased appetite that employees have for working off-site – 'Don't make me go back to "hard pants" five days a week' (*Financial Times*, 5 June 2021c).

Subsequent chapters in this book will provide a much fuller review of the historical and contemporary evidence on all of these matters. These headlines do, however, provide a foretaste of the issues reviewed by this book and backed up by empirical and theoretical evidence.

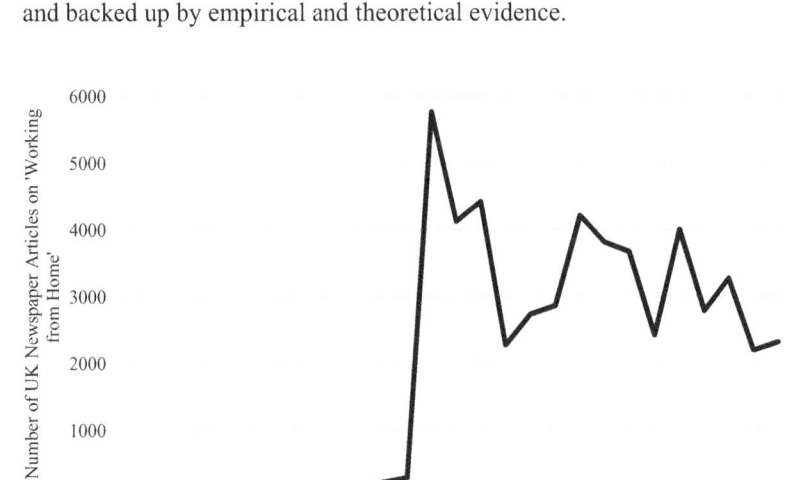

Figure 1.1 UK Newspaper Articles on 'Working from Home', March 2019–May 2021
Source: Extracted from Nexis.com, own calculations.

The spike in homeworking has ignited worldwide interest from employers, employees, and politicians alike. For example, Google searches of terms such as 'homeworking', 'working at home', and 'working from home' jumped as governments across the globe introduced restrictions and encouraged working at home wherever possible. In mid to late March 2020, searches using one of these three phrases were at their peak and were roughly ten times as popular as before the outbreak of coronavirus. The popularity of these searches has since declined. Nevertheless, they still remain twice as popular as similar searches carried out before Covid-19 (see Figure 1.2).

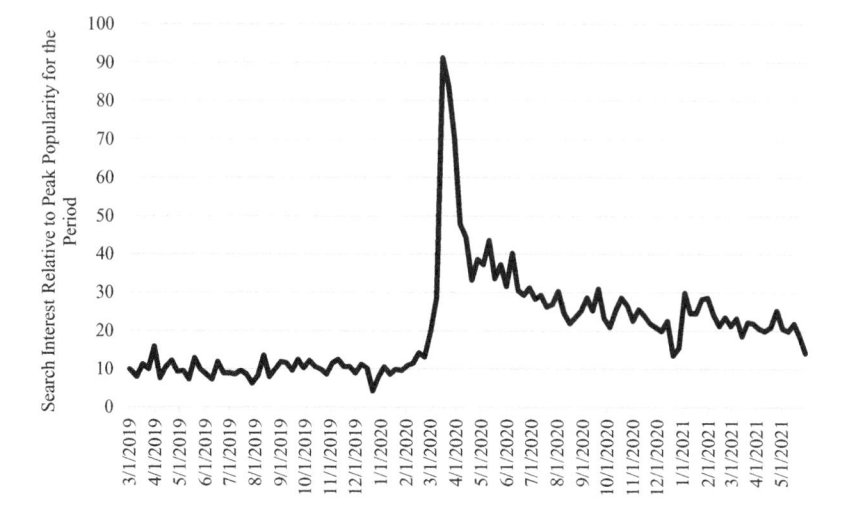

Figure 1.2 Google Worldwide Searches of 'Homeworking', 'Working at Home', and 'Working from Home', January 2019–May 2021

Source: Extracted from Google Trends, own calculations.

All academic debates have their twists and turns. However, the study of where work is carried out has more than its fair share. A key aim of this book is to chart the evolution of that debate and to situate the plethora of terms used to highlight particular changes to the spatial location of work. These include similar sounding, but conceptually distinctive terms such as 'remote working', 'working at home', 'homeworking', 'working from home', 'mobile working', and 'hybrid working'.

The aim of this chapter is to start to put the current interest in the shifting location of work into a historical context. It therefore briefly outlines the debates and issues dominating the field before the outbreak of coronavirus, and the debates and issues prompted by the experience of lengthy, often enforced, periods of homeworking with little or no physical access to the office. In particular, the chapter highlights a significant shift in the type of 'homeworker' under discussion, the pre-pandemic interest in 'mobile working', and the post-pandemic appeal of 'remote' and 'hybrid' working.

1.2 Pre-coronavirus Debates and Issues

It should be made clear at the onset that carrying out work at home is not new, far from it. Prior to industrialisation, households were not only places of social reproduction but also locations in which much production took place. Farms, workshops, manor houses, and palaces were household economies. As a result, domestic and economic relationships were closely integrated; home and work were not separate spheres of social and economic life. Farmers and rural labourers occupied the same buildings as agricultural machinery and livestock. Apprentices slept beside their benches in their masters' workshops.

As a result of the industrial revolution, two new relatively autonomous sets of relations came into being (Humphries, 1982; Boxer and Quataert, 2000). The home focused on consumption and the reproduction of labour, while the workplace was devoted to the production of goods and services for sale. As a result, most people left home to go to work and, at the end of the working day, left work to return home. The relationship between the times and spaces of work and non-work became linear, sequential, and chronological. In the main, household relations ceased to be linked to economic production. The separation of the home from the workplace also meant work was no longer an integral part of family life, but a separate external activity.

Although the onset of industrialisation meant that the majority of workers were engaged in work activities outside the home, the domestic sphere remained an important workplace for a number of occupational groups. For example, lawyers and doctors often gave advice and treated patients at home. Similarly, some working-class jobs (especially those performed by women) continued to take place in the home (Davidoff and Hall, 1987; Boris, 1994). For many years, home-located workers engaged in routine manual and industrial tasks were a neglected and exploited group (Boris and Prügl, 1996). Official surveys and censuses tended to undercount their numbers, employers paid them rock-bottom wages, trade unionists treated them as unwelcome competitors to factory-based workers, and business analysts regarded them as a backward and declining anomaly in a modern economy. They were an invisible workforce hidden from public view, but located in the private sphere of the home. Many were women with young children. Migrant and ethnic minority communities were also heavily involved (Boris and Prügl, 1996; Allen and Wolkowitz, 1987; Phizacklea, 1990; Phizacklea and Wolkowitz, 1995; Felstead and Jewson, 2000).

There were, of course, practical limitations to the type of work that could be carried out at home but such restrictions were, to some extent, historically and culturally specific. For example, in the late nineteenth century, nail-making and chain-making in Britain were predominately carried out in people's homes. At that time, around half of all British nails and chains were produced in domestic premises in and around Birmingham (Bythell, 1978).

In the 1990s, homeworking was still conventionally thought of as primarily involving manual jobs carried out in manufacturing industry and routine service occupations (Huws, 1994). These included those working in the boot and shoe trade, and clothing industry as well as packers and assemblers of items such as Christmas crackers, handbags, nappies, and children's toys (see Felstead and Jewson, 2000: Table 1.1). Policy debates of the time were heavily influenced by this image of homeworking. For example, *Homeworker (Protection) Bills* were presented to the UK Parliament four times – in 1978, 1981, 1991, and 1996. While none of them became law, the issues facing homeworkers were publicly aired. All four bills aimed to ensure that homeworkers were treated as employees and were therefore entitled to protection against low pay, unfair treatment, and poor working conditions.

Legislation at the time was also framed with this image of homeworking in mind. For example, until 1996, employers were required by the *Factories Act 1961* to register 'homeworkers' with the local authority. Here, 'homeworkers' were defined as those carrying out certain types of work at home. Although these included activities such as sewing garments, making stuffed toys, and assembling Christmas crackers, they also covered activities commonly found in factories in the early part of the twentieth century – for example, the making of iron chains, cables, and anchors (Felstead, 1996). Its conceptualisation of homeworking, therefore, focused on historically specific manufacturing activities. This section of the act was repealed in 1996 as this type of homeworking was considered to be of less relevance to the UK in the twenty-first century.

This group of home workers faded from view in subsequent debates, with their plight only occasionally reported (e.g. Homeworkers Worldwide, 2013). This can be seen in the rise and fall of local groups set up to provide help, support, and advice services to these particular homeworkers. This included providing them with information packs on employment, welfare benefits, and other rights free of charge and on demand. A telephone hotline on which homeworkers could get free advice was also commonly provided. Newsletters were produced and circulated to existing contacts as well as community and advice centres. The more developed and well-resourced groups were able to print both Fact Packs and Newsletters in several languages, thereby expanding their reach. In addition, some local groups did, on occasion, run training programmes designed to give homeworkers the self-confidence to progress to other programmes and possibly escape from homeworking altogether (Hopkins, 1992; Tate, 1996). However, all this activity was contingent on accessing local resources, often provided by friendly local authorities and, therefore, subject to the vagaries of the political process. This support, and the presumed need for these activities, gradually evaporated. By 2004, campaigns such as the Leicester Outwork Campaign, the Greenwich Homeworkers Project, and the West Yorkshire Homeworking Group had all closed. In 2008, the coordinating organisation of these individual campaigns – the National Group on Homeworking – also closed leaving a still vulnerable group of workers without any dedicated help, support, or representation (Holden, 2011).

By this time, attention had shifted to the twenty-first-century version of homeworking. This refers to office workers who work at home using digital devices, such as a mobile phone, a laptop, and an internet connection to the office and the wider world. Futurologists were confidently predicting that by the start of the new millennium the majority of work would be carried out in 'electronic cottages' with an 'emphasis on the home as the centre of society' (Toffler, 1980: 210). It was estimated that by 2010 '40 to 50% of the work activities of many managerial and professional activities are likely to be undertaken at home' (Scase, 1999: 28). Other estimates suggested that around 32% of the entire UK workforce would be working at home by 2006 (estimates reported by Lees, 1999: 16). However, even using a broad interpretation of 'homeworking', these predictions were well wide of the mark. For example, the use of the home as a place of work for at least one day a week was estimated to be around 13% in 2002, falling far short of what futurologists were predicting (Felstead *et al.*, 2003: Table 1).

Faced with this evidence, attention pivoted away from the idea that the home would become the future of work to one where work was spatially fluid. It was therefore predicted that 'for a substantial proportion of workers, work in 20 years' time will be more about movement than staying put' (Moynagh and Worsly, 2005: 101). The study of mobility therefore became fashionable (e.g. Urry, 2000; chapter 3). As a consequence, researchers became fascinated by work carried out while on the move and in a variety of places outside of the conventional workplace or the home. These transitional places of work included the car, the train, and the plane as well as stop-over points used while travelling. Examples of these 'third places' included motorway service stations, hotel lobbies, and airport lounges from where work can be carried out (Burchell *et al.*, 2021; Ojala and Pyöriä, 2018; Vartiainen and Hyrkkänen, 2010; Hislop and Axtell, 2007; Felstead *et al.*, 2005). Information technology greatly facilitated the freeing of work from place. Mobile phones, laptops, email, the Internet, and wireless connections enabled more and more work – and office work in particular – to be carried out wherever workers happen to be and whatever the time (hence the notion of 'teleworking'). However, both working at home and mobile working were growing at a much slower pace before the Covid-19 pandemic than many of the heady predictions would suggest (see Chapter 3).

1.3 Coronavirus-Inspired Debates and Issues

The restrictions placed on citizens around the world and calls for individuals to work at home, if they can, shifted the focus of research yet again. For months on end, many workers were caged in their own homes and their mobility was severely restricted. Much of the coronavirus research has therefore focused on work that can be detached from the workplace and relocated into the home lock, stock, and barrel.

Economists, for example, examined how feasible it is for jobs to be carried out at home. Researchers in the US have classified 867 different types of jobs according to whether or not they can be done at home (Dingel and Neiman, 2020: 3). The allocation process is based on responses given by job holders to surveys carried out by the US Bureau of Labor Statistics (BLS). A total of 15 conditions have to be met for jobs to be considered appropriate for homeworking. These include the frequency with which email is used, the importance of outdoor work, the frequency of face-to-face interaction, the use of electrical and mechanical equipment, and exposure to hazards. This suggests that around a third of jobs in the US (37%) and a slightly higher proportion of jobs in the UK (43%) could be carried out at home (Adams-Prassl *et al.*, 2020). Furthermore, research in the US suggests that the shift to homeworking in the pandemic was most pronounced among: managerial, professional, and related occupations; geographical areas with a higher share of these occupations; and individuals who possess higher qualifications and receive better pay (Brynjolfsson *et al.*, 2020; Bick *et al.*, 2020). These are individuals with very different characteristics and doing very different jobs to the homeworkers which were the focus of local support groups and campaigns set up to protect them from exploitation by unscrupulous employers. However, the term 'homeworker' is used to refer to both groups in academic, policymaking, and public discourses.

However, despite these shifts and changes, today's homeworkers – and those of times gone by – confront some similar issues, such as the ways in which spatial and temporal boundaries are generated, maintained, and policed. This involves defining and constructing boundaries around the times and spaces devoted to work and home life which, by definition, take place within one locale. Marking spatial boundaries involves deciding where in the home to work – in the spare bedroom, on the living room table, or in the kitchen – and the degree of permanency and exclusivity accorded to these newly constituted places of work. It may also involve decisions such as the location of work equipment and the storage of physical documents. Marking temporal boundaries involves identifying – on a daily, weekly, and longer term basis – divisions between working and non-working times, such as the length of the working day, and the length and timing of breaks.

Both forms of marking behaviour also require negotiation and agreement with other members of the household and are under constant review.

Pre-pandemic research suggests that the experience of combining home and work in these ways differs between men and women (Haddon and Lewis, 1994; Salmi, 1997; Probert and Wacjman, 1988a, 1988b). Men tend to say that they value flexibility in order to coordinate work time and free time, to escape the control of workplace authority, and to enhance their efficiency. Women, on the other hand, are more likely to seek flexibility in order to combine a number of different work demands, such as housework, child care, and paid employment. However, the coronavirus lockdowns required everyone to work at home if they could and for parents to homeschool their children. This placed added pressure on both parents to combine home and work in ways not previously seen. Furthermore, while technology facilitated the move to working at home, it also meant that working hours were increasingly difficult to define. This has led to policy discussions, prompted by trade unions and others, around giving employees the statutory right to disconnect.

Employers also face challenges. Foremost among them is the fear that out of sight, employees will take it easy, and as a consequence employee productivity will fall. This is a long-held belief which, before the pandemic, limited a more extensive roll out of an employee's right to work at home if requested. Coupled with the presumed loss of impromptu learning and creativity, some employers even banned staff from working at home before the pandemic began. However, even reluctant employers had to allow working at home during the pandemic.

Where work is carried out can have societal effects too. A sustained increase in the number of people working at home, for example, may reduce greenhouse gas emissions since it removes the need to travel. Mobile working, on the other hand, requires transportation of one sort or another, with some forms of transport more polluting than others. Recent research suggests that in the US road vehicles are the biggest culprit, accounting for a whopping 82% of emissions while air travel produces 9% and rail is responsible for just 2% (US Environmental Protection Agency, 2021). Not surprisingly, therefore, governments and organisations across the world see the long-term use of working at home as one of the ways in which they might be able to reduce their carbon footprint.

1.4 Reading Guide

Each chapter in the book can be read independently of the others. So, there is no need to read the chapters in order and entire chapters can be skipped. In addition, each chapter offers a self-contained synthesis of existing evidence with its own set of references. This is designed to help teachers who might recommend certain chapters to students and/or those who want a quick overview of a particular theme. Throughout this book, references will be made to how the debate on the location of work has evolved from the latter part of the twentieth century to the present day. It will therefore offer a 'then and now' comparison, drawing on the UK experience in particular. These contrasts will be particularly pronounced in the following two chapters given the shifting focus of the debate.

Chapter 2 – *Defining Remote Working* – considers the definitions of terms frequently – and imprecisely – used to characterise the location of work. It has been common for politicians, commentators, and practitioners to refer to the need for people to work *from* home if they can. For example, on 22 September 2020, Boris Johnson, the Prime Minister, addressed the nation in a live TV interview where he once again asked 'office workers to work from home if they can' (Prime Minister's Statement, 22 September 2020; Cabinet Office, 2020). However, workers have actually been advised to limit their mobility; that is, to work *at* home and not to venture from the home if at all possible. The easing of coronavirus restrictions has led to more spatial movement with 'remote working' often used to describe work that can be carried out in a *variety of places* outside the premises of the employer – for example, in the local coffee shop, in a co-working hub, in a hotel lobby, or while travelling. 'Hybrid working', too, has become popularly discussed and captures the idea that employees are enabled to *work part of the time* on the employer's premises and part of the time off-site either at home or anywhere of their choosing.

Chapter 3 – *Trends in Remote Working* – considers how the location of work has been evolving since the 1980s with a notable spike in working at home as a result of the pandemic. The chapter also considers how the demographic make-up of those involved and the jobs they do has changed over time. The policy debates, too, have changed. Concerns about protecting employees, particularly women and ethnic minorities, against low pay, unfair treatment, and poor working conditions have been displaced by other issues. Now, debates about the right to work at home from day one and the right to disconnect have taken centre stage as the appetite to work at home has risen, and the boundaries between home and work have become increasingly blurred.

Chapter 4 – *Remote Working and the Employer* – assesses the costs and benefits to employers of allowing, and even encouraging, their employees to carry out more of their work off-site. Doing so upends traditional management approaches which have been incorporated into the architectural design of offices. These features include open-plan seating, internal glass walls, and large central atriums. These architectural features reflect and constitute a managerial approach that relies on making employees both 'visible' and 'present'. Visibility refers to the ability of managers, supervisors, and work colleagues to observe employees at work. The physical presence of employees on-site enhances the potential for them to participate – intentionally and/ or serendipitously – in relations with their peers and others in acts of learning, social bonding, and building organisational camaraderie. The chapter draws on the theoretical and empirical literature to examine the pros and cons of shifts in the location of work. It also considers the challenges that the declining significance of the single workplace has for those managing an increasingly dispersed workforce.

Chapter 5 – *Remote Working and the Employee* – considers the effects on employees. After all, working at home has often been promoted and sought by employees as a means of readjusting their work–life balance and raising their well-being. However, some employees find that bringing work into the home makes it more difficult to draw these boundaries, especially in certain circumstances. These include: when employees are told to work at home because of a national health emergency; when space at home is limited and used by other household members; and/or when homeworking jobs are the only ones available. Other issues may also arise. Those working off-site may get overlooked for promotion, have fewer opportunities to engage in training and development, work in less safe environments with poorer equipment, and suffer from lengthening working days and more intensive working hours. This chapter reviews the evidence along with some of the most notable policy responses. High on this list is the debate around the right to disconnect. This gives public recognition that the 'always on' culture makes drawing the line between home and work increasingly difficult, even when office employees are no longer required to be physically present in the office.

Chapter 6 – *The Future of Remote Working* – speculates about the long-lasting legacy of what some have called 'the great homeworking experiment'. While not a true experiment, given the lack of a control group, working at home has been a new experience for many. Some have relished the opportunity; others have hated it. Employers are similarly divided. There have been pluses and minuses, too, for society. Pollution levels fell during the pandemic as fewer people used motorised travel to get to and from work. On the other hand, fewer office workers in cities reduced trade for city centre businesses such as bars, restaurants, and cafés. If more work is carried out at home in the future, this will have implications for city and town planning. These are all issues that will need to be tackled since there appears little prospect of completely turning the clock back to pre-pandemic ways of working. Instead, 'remote working' – the detachment of work from the traditional workplace – and 'hybrid working' – allowing employees to pick and mix where they work – are likely to characterise the future of work in the years ahead.

References

Adams-Prassl, A, Boneva, T, Golin, M and Rauh, C (2020) *Work Tasks That Can Be Done from Home: Evidence of the Variation Within and Across Occupations and Industries*, Cambridge Working Papers in Economics, No. 2040, Cambridge: University of Cambridge.

Allen, S and Wolkowitz, C (1987) *Homeworking: Myths and Realities*, London: Palgrave Macmillan.

BBC News (2020) 'Google tells staff to work at home because of coronavirus', 11 March, www.bbc.co.uk/news/technology-51828782 (accessed 17 March 2021).

Bick, A, Blandin, A and Mertens, K (2020) *Work from Home After the COVID-19 Outbreak*, Federal Bank of Dallas Working Paper, No. 2017, Dallas: Federal Bank of Dallas.

Boris, E (1994) *Home to Work: Motherhood and the Politics of Industrial Homework in the United States*, Cambridge: Cambridge University Press.

Boris, E and Prügl, E (1996) *Homeworkers in Global Perspective: Invisible No More*, London: Routledge.

Boxer, M J and Quataert, J H (eds) (2000) *Connecting Spheres: European Women in a Globalizing World, 1500 to the Present* (2nd Edition), Oxford: Oxford University Press.

Brynjolfsson, E, Horton, J, Ozimek, A, Rock, D, Sharma, G and TuYe, H-Y (2020) *Covid-19 and Remote Work: An Early Look at US Data*, NBER Working Paper Series, Working Paper, No. 27344, Cambridge, MA: National Bureau of Economic Research.

Burchell, B, Reuschke, D and Zhang, M (2021) 'Spatial and temporal segmenting of urban workplaces: the gendering of multi-locational working', *Urban Studies*, 58(11): 2207–2232.

Bythell, D (1978) *The Sweated Trades: Outwork in Nineteenth Century Britain*, London: Batsford Academic.

Cabinet Office (2020) *Coronavirus (COVID-19): What Has Changed*, London: Cabinet Office, 22 September, www.gov.uk/government/news/coronavirus-covid-19-what-has-changed-22-september (accessed 5 October 2020).

Daily Mail (2020) 'Empty offices are killing town centre, by Jason Groves and Henry Martin', *Daily Mail*, 10 July.

Davidoff, L and Hall, C (1987) *Family Fortunes: Men and Women of the English Middle Class, 1970–1850*, London: Hutchinson.

Dingel, J I and Neiman, B (2020) *How Many Jobs Can Be Done at Home?*, NBER Working Paper Series, Working Paper, No. 26948, Cambridge, MA: National Bureau of Economic Research.

Eurofound (2020) *Living, Working and COVID-19*, Luxembourg: Publications of the European Union.

Felstead, A (1996) 'Homeworking in Britain: the national picture in the mid-1990s', *Industrial Relations Journal*, 27(3): 225–238.

Felstead, A and Jewson, N (2000) *In Work, at Home: Towards an Understanding of Homeworking*, London: Routledge.

Felstead, A, Jewson, N and Walters, S (2003) *The Changing Place of Work*, ESRC Future of Work Programme, Working Paper, No. 28, Leeds: University of Leeds, June.

Felstead, A, Jewson, N and Walters, S (2005) *Changing Places of Work*, London: Palgrave Macmillan.

Financial Times (2020a) 'Homeworking is depriving me of juicy gossip, by Emma Jacobs', *Financial Times*, 13 July.

Financial Times (2020b) 'Death of the office exaggerated despite the homeworking boom' by Javier Espinoza', *Financial Times*, 1 July.

Financial Times (2021a) 'Homeworking spells gloom for Canary Wharf, by George Hammond', *Financial Times*, 11 January.

Financial Times (2021b) 'Offices: homeworking will save employers billions, by Helen Thomas', *Financial Times*, 8 April.

Financial Times (2021c) 'Don't make me go back to "hard pants" five days a week, by Pilita Clark', *Financial Times*, 5 June.

Haddon, L and Lewis, A (1994) 'The experience of teleworking: an annotated review', *The International Journal of Human Resource Management*, 5(1): 195–223.

Hislop, D and Axtell, C (2007) 'The neglect of spatial mobility in contemporary studies of work: the case of telework', *New Technology, Work and Employment*, 22(1): 34–51.

Holden, N (2011) *Homeworking: Here and Now*, Leeds: Homeworkers Worldwide.

Homeworkers Worldwide (2013) *Homeworking in the UK: A Practical and Ethical Guide for Businesses*, Leeds: Homeworkers Worldwide.

Hopkins, M (1992) 'Empowerment or escape? Technical training for homeworkers in Britain', in Mitter, S (ed) *Computer-Aided Manufacturing and Women's Employment: The Clothing Industry in Four EC Countries*, Berlin: Springer-Verlag.

Humphries, J (1982) 'Class struggle and the persistence of the working-class family', in Giddens, A and Held, D (eds) *Class, Power and Conflict*, Basingstoke: Palgrave Macmillan.

Huws, U (1994) *Home Truths: Results from a National Survey of Homeworkers*, Leeds: National Group on Homeworking.

ILO (2020) *Working from Home: Estimating the Worldwide Potential*, ILO Brief, Geneva: International Labour Office, April.

Lees, C (1999) 'The age of the homeworker?', in Myerson, J (ed) *Work at Home: The Proceedings of the Thinktank on Home-Working at the Royal College of Art*, London: Royal College of Art.

London Standard (2021) 'Where were the homeworking hotspots in 2020?' by Henry Saker-Clark', *London Standard*, 17 May.

Moynagh, M and Worsely, R (2005) *Working in the Twenty-First Century*, King's Lynn: The Tomorrow Project.

OECD (2020) *Policy Responses to the COVID-19 Crisis*, Paris: Organisation for Economic Co-Operation and Development.

Ojala, S and Pyöriä, P (2018) 'Mobile knowledge workers and traditional mobile workers: assessing the prevalence of multi-locational work in Europe', *Acta Sociologica*, 61(4): 402–418.

Phizacklea, A (1990) *Unpacking the Fashion Industry: Gender, Racism and Class in Production*, London: Routledge.

Phizacklea, A and Wolkowitz, C (1995) *Homeworking Women: Gender, Ethnicity and Class at Work*, London: Sage.

Probert, B and Wacjman, J (1988a) 'New technology outwork', in Willis, E (ed) *Technology and the Labour Process: Australian Case Studies*, Sydney: Allen and Unwin.

Probert, B and Wacjman, J (1988b) 'Technological change and the future of work', *Journal of Industrial Relations*, 30(2): 432–448.

Salmi, M (1997) 'Autonomy and time in home-based work', in Heiskanen, T and Rantalaiho, L (eds) *Gendered Practices in Working Life*, London: Palgrave Macmillan.

Scase, R (1999) *Britain Towards 2010: The Changing Business Environment*, London: Department for Trade and Industry.

Tate, J (1996) 'Making links: the growth of homeworker networks', in Boris, E and Prügl, E (eds) *Homeworkers in Global Perspective: Invisible No More*, London: Routledge.

The Daily Telegraph (2021) 'Homeworkers get more done during pandemic, study finds, by Tom Rees', *The Daily Telegraph*, 1 April.

The Daily Telegraph (2020) 'Gentler, greener, quieter: welcome to the city of the future, by Chris Moss', *The Daily Telegraph*, 1 December.

The Guardian (2021) 'Homeworking sounds good – until your job takes over your life, by John Harris', *The Guardian*, 7 March.

The Independent (2021) 'Homeworking isn't working, at least for the young, by Hamish McRae', *The Independent*, 24 March.

Toffler, A (1980) *The Third Wave*, New York: William Morrow.

Urry, J (2000) *Sociology Beyond Societies: Mobilities for the Twenty-First Century*, London: Routledge.

US Environmental Protection Agency (2021) *Fast Facts: US Transportation Sector Greenhouse Emissions, 1990–2019*, Washington, DC: Office of Transportation and Air Quality.

Vartiainen, M and Hyrkkänen, U (2010) 'Changing requirements and mental workload factors in mobile multi-locational work', *New Technology, Work and Employment*, 25(2): 117–135.

2 Defining Remote Working

'When *I* use a word', Humpty Dumpty said in a rather scornful tone, 'it means just what I choose it to mean – neither more nor less'. 'The question is', said Alice, 'whether you can make words mean so many different things', Lewis Carroll *Through the Looking Glass*, first published in 1871.

2.1 Introduction

A key feature of the traditional factory or office is the allocation of individual workers to particular premises and even specific locations within them. In fact, this is the origin of the non-hyphenated term 'workplace'; that is, a place where paid work is done. The principle of allocating every person to a place and every place to a person is embedded in traditional workplace design – the layout of factories and the use of assembly lines, and the floor plans of offices and the arrangement of desks. 'Placing' workers in factories or offices, and in particular places within them, makes the security of materials and regulation of workflows much simpler. More subtly, it allows for the use of disciplinary devices associated with panoptical surveillance, the normalising gaze, and the regimentation of time (Thompson, 1967; Foucault, 1977; Thrift, 1990; Bain and Taylor, 2000). In line with these developments, the term 'office' acquired an additional meaning. While it once only referred to a high-status position or function, it now also refers to a type of workplace where managerial, professional, and administrative work is done. Typically, these jobs involve sitting at a desk, hence the colloquial phrase 'desk jobs'.

However, the placement of work into traditional offices and factories following industrialisation has never been wholly complete; some work has continued to be done at home. Homeworking, in some shape or form, has therefore remained a feature of the UK economy for centuries. This is especially the case in the clothing and footwear industries even when the putting out system was in decline and factories were on the rise. Marx referred

DOI: 10.4324/9781003247050-2

to the 'invisible threads' between the two with the homeworking labour force acting as 'an external department of the manufacturers, warehouses and even of the workshops of the smaller masters' (Marx quoted in Allen and Wolkowitz, 1987: 18). Furthermore, in World War II, homeworking was actively encouraged by government with women urged to do their bit for the war effort by assembling aircraft parts at home, while their husbands were fighting on the frontline (Summerfield, 1989).

Taking an overview perspective, there are two images of homeworking: one draws on a largely historic account and the other focuses on a more contemporary account of office work carried out at home. The historic image is one of low-paid, low-skilled manual work carried out in cramped, dingy, and unsafe surroundings, sometimes involving child labour. The image of today's homeworker, on the other hand, focuses on office work carried out by much better paid workers who have typically gone to the office five days a week and worked 9–5, or what are referred to as 'office hours'. Photographic imaginary of these contrasting archetypes is often used in newspaper articles, blogs, and substantive research reports (e.g. Gottlieb *et al.*, 2020; ILO, 2021).

The aim of this chapter is to outline conceptual ways of differentiating between these archetypes as well as identifying other places where work can be carried out. It will also provide conceptual distinctions between terms that litter the debate and sometimes confuse rather than clarify understanding. These include the term 'homeworking' itself as well as 'working at home', 'working from home', 'mobile working', 'remote working', and 'hybrid working'. While this will equip readers to make important distinctions, it is equally important to highlight that commentary and debate are not always rigorous. Throughout the book, for example, the terms used by authors will be used, although their use does not always correspond to the conceptual distinctions outlined in what follows.

This chapter focuses on the different types of places in which work may be undertaken, the amount of time spent working in these places, and the type of occupations and industries involved. These distinctions lie at the heart of the conceptual fault lines between terms. These include, for example, the distinction between working at home and working from home, and the difference between remote and hybrid working. However, slippery use of these terms is common, making comparisons between research results hazardous; even though the same words are used, 'like for like' comparisons may not always be possible. The aim of this chapter, therefore, is to make readers aware of the differences and therefore provide a framework for judging how comparable they really are. Examination of survey questions used to gather data on the location of work will be used to illustrate these differences in action. Throughout the book, we will also alert readers to these differences when reviewing the research evidence, but would strongly urge readers to be equally vigilant when reading the evidence themselves. This applies especially to the more historical accounts which focus on a particular type of homeworker very different from the homeworkers of today. As Alice reminds us in the quote at the top of this chapter, the *same words* can mean so many *different things*. Moreover, these meanings can *change over time*.

2.2 Placing Work

At the outset, a preliminary, but crucial, conceptual distinction needs to be made with respect to whether work is done in the home; within the grounds of the home; or whether the home is used as a base from which work is done. In each of these three scenarios, the extent to which work is spatially located within the home varies, often substantially. It is vital therefore to distinguish between people who:

- work *at home* (e.g. someone, such as the author of this book, who does their research and delivers lectures, at least during the pandemic, while sitting in a converted spare bedroom);
- work *in the same grounds and buildings as home* (e.g. a farmer, a pub landlord, or a bed and breakfast proprietor); and
- work *from home* (e.g. a plumber or an electrician who carries out jobs on a building site, in a factory, or in other people's homes, but uses his/her home as a base).

Although this division may at first sight seem straightforward, it routinely leads to conceptual confusion. This leads to the non-comparability of many data sets, the production of varying estimates of 'homeworking', and differences in terms of who is involved and what type of work they do.

This is because work and home overlap to varying degrees depending on whether work is done *at* home, in the *same grounds and buildings* as home, or *from* home. This means that people who work from home or in buildings attached but separate from their home – such as a shed, garage, or barn – undertake their work activities away from the spatial location where domestic work is also carried out. This includes a plumber who takes the odd one or two telephone calls at home to make appointments, but who does most of his plumbing work in other people's homes.

Similarly, a pub landlord is able to separate her work from her home life by serving drinks and chatting to regulars in the bar while living in a self-contained flat above the pub. However, in some pubs, these lines are blurred. For example, the sitting room often doubles up as a place where staff meet and the family congregates, and the kitchen is used to make meals for clients and the family. The blurring of these lines is amply illustrated in the fictional pub – The Rovers Return – in the ITV soap opera *Coronation Street*. Here, family dramas are played out in public view in the bar as well as in the supposedly private living room, bedrooms, and kitchen, which are normally, but not always, off-limits to non-household members.

Working at home, on the other hand, means that the overlap is complete; paid work is done in the private sphere of the home where childcare, cooking, and cleaning are also carried out. Such workers experience the full force of the conflicting pressures of the world of work and home. As a consequence, they and their fellow household members have to manage, reconcile, and accommodate these pressures.

The conceptual divides between home and work are reflected in some of the survey instruments used to track the changing location of work. For example, in 1981, the annual Labour Force Survey (LFS) carried, for the first time, a question on where respondents worked. Respondents were asked, 'do you work mainly' in one of four locations: 'in your own home; in the same buildings or grounds as your home; in different places using home as a base; or do you work somewhere quite different from home?' Despite offering a unique perspective on the location of work in the UK, 11 years were to pass before the question was repeated. Presumably, it was dropped because it was not considered to be of interest. Nevertheless, it reappeared in 1992 and has been asked in every quarterly LFS ever since. Other homeworking-related questions have been added, and subsequently removed, over the years. These include questions identifying where people worked in the week before the interview as well as questions on whether the use of a computer and a telephone were necessary for respondents to work at or from home (see Table 2.1).

By definition, individual-level surveys, such as the LFS, are based on samples of the population with considerable effort devoted to ensuring that they are representative. Only relatively rarely are questions asked of, and information gathered on, all those living in the UK. The Census of Population is the exception to this rule; it covers everyone and has to be completed by law. It is the only poll that provides a detailed picture of the entire population and is unique because it covers everyone living in the UK on a particular day and asks the same core questions of everyone, no matter where they live.

The obvious advantage of the Census is its comprehensive coverage. The other major benefit is that it paints a picture of the human geography of the UK at a very fine level of spatial disaggregation. Whereas other individual-level sources can provide insights at the national, regional, and sometimes local authority levels, the Census goes much further in that it

Table 2.1 Labour Force Survey Questions, 1981–2021

Question	Frequency
Main Work Location '(In your main job) do you work mainly . . . • in your own home • in the same grounds and buildings as your home • in different places using home as a base • or somewhere quite separate from home?'	Asked in 1981, then spring and autumn quarters from spring 1992 to winter 1996/7. Every seasonal quarter thereafter. Then, asked every calendar quarter when the LFS moved to calendar quarters in 2006. This question was asked of respondents' main and second jobs.
Partial Work Location 'Have you spent at least one FULL day in the seven days ending Sunday the (date) working . . . • in your own home • in the same grounds and buildings as your home • in different places using home as a base • or not worked at home during reference week?'	Initially, it was asked in every spring and autumn quarter from spring 1997 to winter 1997/8. But from then, it was asked in the spring quarter only. In 2006, it was asked in the second quarter when the LFS moved to calendar quarters. This question was asked of respondents' main and second jobs. However, in 2015, the question was only asked of those responding to wave 1 of the quarter 2 survey (each survey consists of five waves). This reduced the sample size drastically. Furthermore, these data are not publicly available. However, since 2020, the question has been asked of all respondents to the quarter 3 survey.
Sometimes Work at Home Do you ever do any paid or unpaid work at home for your (main) job? • Yes • No	Asked in spring and autumn quarters since spring 1992 until winter 1997/8. Asked only once a year thereafter in the spring seasonal quarter. Then, in the second quarter when, in 2006, the LFS moved to calendar quarters. This question was only asked of respondents' main job. The question was dropped in 2016.
Use of Technology to Support Working at/From Home Do you use both a telephone *and* a computer to carry out your work at home? • Yes • No	Every spring and autumn quarters from spring 1997 to winter 1997/8. Asked only once a year thereafter in the spring seasonal quarter. Then, in the second quarter when, in 2006, the LFS moved to calendar quarters. Only asked of main job and those who work at home or use home as a base on either a one day a week or mainly basis.

(Continued)

Table 2.1 (Continued)

Question	Frequency
Would it be possible to work at home (or use home as a base) without using both a telephone and a computer? • Yes • No	Every spring and autumn quarters from spring 1997 to winter 1997/8. Asked only once a year thereafter in the spring seasonal quarter. Then, in the second quarter when, in 2006, the LFS moved to calendar quarters. Only asked of main job and those who work at home or use home as a base on either a one day a week or mainly basis.
Remote Working Do you currently do part or all of your job from home or another remote location? Remote working includes working outside of a traditional office or 'central' place of work. It includes working at home and close to home in your local community, but does not include workers who travel to different sites to perform their duties such as district nurses, door-to-door salespeople, or field interviewers. • Yes • No How many hours do you work from home or another remote location in a usual week? Only asked if respondent reports doing part or all of their job remotely as specified earlier. Asked every quarter since 2021. • Range 0–99 hours	Asked every quarter since 2021.

allows robust analysis to be carried out at ward/postal sector level (Felstead and Jewson, 1995).

Census data on work location have been collected in slightly different ways. Since 1966, these data have been collected in the context of the individual's workplace address and how they travel to that address, such as by car, train, or on foot. Included in the list of possible responses to the 1981 and 1991 Censuses was the option 'works mainly at home'. Since 2001, this option has become 'works mainly at or from home'. This was the formulation used in the 2021 Census. However, the conflation of those who work at home with those who work from home results in imprecision about where paid work is actually carried out. Furthermore, the Census does not differentiate between those working at home as opposed to in the same grounds and buildings as their home. As a result, those who do not travel to work, such as farmers and agricultural workers, appear as 'homeworkers', hence the high rates of 'homeworking' in rural parts of the UK.

These are major drawbacks because a key feature of working at home is the overlap of the worlds of work and domestic life – the experience of being 'in work at home' (Felstead and Jewson, 2000). This is at its greatest when work is carried out in the spaces where people conduct their daily lives – bedrooms, kitchens, dining rooms, and so on. Another problem is that Census data are only collected once every ten years with the results published a year or more after data collection. The full results of the 2021 Census will not be available until March 2023. This further limits the usefulness of the Census as an up-to-date portrayal of the extent of 'homeworking' and its prevalence. However, it does shed some light on the move away from offices and factories as the main place of work for a growing proportion of those in paid work (see Chapter 3).

Some surveys collect data on where people work from a slightly different angle. They ask respondents if they have access to a variety of flexible working arrangements, including working at home. The Employee Rights and Experiences Survey, for example, asks just such a question as well as a question on take-up of the opportunities identified. These data provide the basis on which to paint the profile of those who have the opportunity to work at home and to contrast this with those who do so. The profiles of these two groups may differ. Previous research has shown that access to working at home is restricted to the most privileged while those who take it up tend to be poorer paid, less educated, and in lesser skilled jobs (Felstead *et al.*, 2002).

Existing survey design tends to focus on the role of the home as a place of work. It does not provide data on the extent to which the office is also being used differently, possibly as a base from which to visit clients or as a drop-in centre used from time to time as in the case of hybrid working. Nor does it reveal the full extent to which people are working remotely with little or no physical presence on employers' premises.

One should also bear in mind that even within a single workplace movement may be possible. For example, those with larger houses may be able to set aside a room with all the paraphernalia of the office – a dedicated desk, an office-grade computer connected with good Wi-Fi, and storage for books, reports, and papers – and have the option to work in other parts of the house or even the garden if they wish. However, those in a bedsit apartment do not have these luxuries. As a result, they have to use the same small space for work activities and home life, and therefore engage in time-space shifting behaviours. On the other hand, mobility is likely to be far more frequent and involve longer distances in other workplaces such as office buildings.

At a conceptual level, this suggests that distinctions also need to be made between workstations, workplaces, and workscapes. Workstations refer to the specific location where work is undertaken, such as at a desk in an office, in a meeting room, on the premises of a client, in a car, on a seat in a railway carriage, or in a spare bedroom at home. The term workplace refers to buildings, or other physical constructions, that contain and support one or more workstations. These include not only office blocks and factories but also railway trains, domestic homes, motorway service stations, airport lounges, or any other container where workstations can be set up and work can be carried out. Finally, there are workscapes. These refer to the total network of workplaces and workstations used by workers in the course of their employment. They comprise all the specific sites in which individuals or groups do work tasks as well as, crucially, the channels of communication and transportation that link them together. Thus, for example, the workscape of a university lecturer typically includes the use of workstations, such as lecture theatres, seminar rooms, meeting rooms, libraries, and office desks (Felstead *et al.*, 2005). Travelling between these workstations may also involve visiting different buildings or workplaces and the use of liminal places such as corridors, stairways, coffee bars, common rooms, bookshops, stationery cupboards, lifts, car parks, and pigeonholes (Urry, 2000; Castells, 2000). It is in these liminal places that much important and unintended social interaction may take place – what are sometimes referred to as 'water cooler' moments (Fayard and Weeks, 2007).

2.3 Times of Work

The workscapes that people inhabit may also vary from week to week and even day to day. This means that work may be carried out in a variety of workstations and located across a range of workplaces, including the home, the office, and on the commute to and from work. Capturing this complexity is difficult using survey techniques. However, qualitative studies are much better equipped to track where, when, and how work is carried out away from the traditional cues of the office.

One such classic is an in-depth ethnographic study of six car-based workers who were accompanied ('shadowed') by a research passenger for a week (Laurier and Philo, 1999; Laurier, 2001a, 2001b). It reveals the practices needed to make working on the move possible. First, the timing of certain work activities, such as telephone calls, had to be specified in advance and the boundaries of availability made clear to others. In office buildings, these boundaries can often be marked spatially. Entering the doors of an organisation, for example, is typically regarded as being at work and on display to the scrutiny of others – fellow colleagues and/or clients. Certain behaviour and performances are therefore expected once on the premises and in view of others (Crang, 1994). In the building itself, a jacket on the back of a chair signals to others that the occupant is 'in', but is temporarily unavailable. Signs such as 'do not disturb' and 'meeting in progress' can also be used to signal visually the boundaries over which others should not cross unless invited. Working on the move, on the other hand, requires that boundaries are set differently. In this context, greater reliance is placed on time-based rather than space-based organisation of activities, so that accessibility is determined by when rather than where someone is available (Green, 2002).

Secondly, the study highlights the importance that everyday materials and devices play in making mobile work possible (cf. Gronow and Warde, 2001). These include the mobile phone, laptop, post-it notes, roadmaps, satnav, and other paraphernalia that have to be carried around in order to connect with others. These pre-assembled parts may even have to be adapted in particular ways for car use. For example, post-it notes may be strategically placed within easy reach for note-taking and stuck on the dashboard to prevent forgetfulness, and the parcel shelf in the boot may be dispensed with to make way for a makeshift filing cabinet containing documents that may need to be consulted.

Thirdly, Laurier and Philo (1999) highlight the ways in which the workplace is repaired when things go wrong. Unlike the office, the assembly and reassembly of the work environment make working in a variety of places fragile and more susceptible to breakdowns. Strategies and tactics to cope with disruptions and interruptions have to be devised as they arise. For example, the short battery life of built-in laptop power supplies may necessitate periodic and planned stops to known power sockets for resupply. Appointment schedules may have to be revised due to unforeseen traffic and weather conditions. The frequent loss of mobile phone connections, due to interference or a poor signal, requires that those working on the move devise an unwritten and unspoken etiquette about who should re-contact who and when.

Surveys cannot reflect the lived experience of what is needed to work outside of the environment of employer-controlled places of work such as the office. In particular, what actions are needed to compensate for the deficiencies of these environments, and, at the same time, mould their work activities around what is possible in different venues. In short, those working remotely have to make places work and allocate work to places. Such an analysis directs attention to the active and creative processes entailed in working in a variety of places, and sheds light on how workers go about 'doing' their daily tasks.

Nevertheless, surveys can shed some light on the amount of time workers spend using different places of work (see Table 2.2). Both the Census

Table 2.2 Examples of Worker-Level Survey Questions

Worker-Level Surveys	Question
Labour Force Survey	'(In your main job) do you work mainly in your own home; in the same grounds and buildings as your home; in different places using home as a base; or somewhere quite separate from home?'
Census	'How do you usually travel to work? Tick one box only. Tick the box for the longest part, *by distance*, of your usual journey to work'. Options given: 'Work mainly at or from home'; 'Underground, metro, light rail, tram'; 'Train'; 'Bus, minibus, or coach'; 'Motorcycle, scooter, or moped'; 'Driving a car or van'; 'Passenger in a car or van'; 'Bicycle'; 'On foot'; and 'Other'.
Skills and Employment Survey	'In your job, where do you mainly work? Please answer from this card. A. At home; B. In the same grounds and buildings as home (e.g. in adjoining property or surrounding land); C. At a single workplace away from home (e.g. office, factory, or shop); D. In a variety of different places of work (e.g. working on clients' premises or in their homes); E. Working on the move (e.g. delivering products or people to different places)'.
Understanding Society	'Do you work mainly . . . At home; At your employer's premises; Driving or travelling around; Or at one or more other places?'
European Working Conditions Survey	'Where is your main place of work? My employers'/my own business' premises (office, factory, shop, school, etc.); Clients' premises; A car or another vehicle; An outside site (construction site, agricultural field, streets of a city); My own home; or Other'.
Understanding Society Covid-19 Study	'During the last four weeks, how often did you work at home? Always; Often; Sometimes; or Never'.
Labour Market Survey	'Did you do any working from home in the week Monday [date] to Sunday [date, year]? Yes; No'.
Opinions and Lifestyle Survey	'In the past seven days, have you worked from home because of the coronavirus (Covid-19) outbreak? Yes; No; Not able to'.
Living, Working and Covid-19	'Have you started to work from home as a result of the Covid-19 situation? Yes; No'.
National Survey for Wales (telephone monthly)	'How much of your work can you do from home? None, some, most, or all?'

Note: For a similar mapping of surveys from across the world, see ILO, 2021: 38–39.

and the LFS, for example, ask respondents to think about where they mainly work. This 'on the whole' frame of reference is used by other surveys such as the Skills and Employment Survey, the European Working Conditions Survey, and Understanding Society (Felstead and Henseke, 2017; Eurofound, 2012; Wheatley, 2017). A different approach is to ask respondents where they were working immediately before being surveyed. The period can be specific, such as during the last week or over the last four weeks, or less specific, such as since the Covid-19 pandemic began. The Labour Market Survey is an example of the former, while the Living, Working and Covid-19 Survey is an example of the latter (Beavan-Seymour, 2020a, 2020b; Eurofound, 2020). Respondents may also be asked the extent to which they work at home – always, often, sometimes, or never as in the case of the Understanding Society Covid-19 Study (Felstead and Reuschke, 2021).

However, some surveys have asked how often respondents have worked in a range of possible work locations over a 12-month period. The EWCS 2015, for example, adopted this approach. Using these data, researchers have been able to piece together a complex picture of the spatio-temporal patterns of work. At its most extreme, the results show that virtually no women work exclusively in vehicles. Men are also more likely to work outside than women and are more likely to work in multiple locations (Burchell *et al.*, 2021).

Another tactic is to ask respondents to estimate what proportion of their work can be done at home. The telephone version of the National Survey for Wales adopts this approach. It has also been adopted in one-off surveys designed to collect real-time information on the impact of the pandemic. For example, Adams-Pressl *et al.* (2020) carried out two surveys in the UK and the US in early March and early April 2020. Around 4,000 workers aged 18 and above took part in each of the four surveys. Respondents were asked to report on a scale ranging from 0 to 100% the share of their tasks they could, if necessary, do at home.

However, a drawback of all of these surveys is that they fail to capture the complexity of the workscapes that workers inhabit in terms of the places they use to work and the times they spend in each of these places. That said, time use surveys do have the potential to provide some of these insights, thereby complementing qualitative studies which shadow one or two workers as they go about their daily tasks. One such survey is the American Time Use Survey (ATUS), which has been carried out by the BLS on an annual basis since 2003. It provides nationally representative estimates of how, where, and with whom Americans spend their time. Respondents are asked by telephone to report on their previous day's activities. These activities are wide-ranging, but crucially for our purposes, they include the amount of time spent on paid work. Respondents are also asked where these activities were carried out and for how long. The places listed are quite limited, but the list does include the respondent's home, their employer's premises, someone else's home, restaurant/bar, and outdoors. These data have been used to estimate the number of pre-pandemic hours workers spent working at home in the US and the occupational and industrial characteristics of those involved (Hensvik *et al.*, 2020).

Similar time use surveys have been carried out more sporadically in the UK. The first was in 2000–2001, the second in 2014–2015, and the third and fourth were carried out more recently in April 2020 and September 2020, respectively. However, in the 2020 surveys, paid work was linked to a limited number of locations, such as 'working from home' or 'working from a café or other workspace'. The results suggest that those working from home tended to start and finish work later than those working elsewhere (Martin, 2021). Further research may be possible using such diary data, hence shedding light on when and where work is undertaken. More sophisticated questioning may also allow future researchers insights into the kaleidoscope of times and spaces where work is carried out.

2.4 Types of Work

Aside from the recent spike of interest in working at home, prompted by the need to prevent the spread of coronavirus, the other major spike of interest was in the last three decades of the twentieth century. This earlier interest was prompted by studies that showed that homeworkers' pay was low, measured against workers doing similar jobs and against standard indices of low pay. This paints a very different picture of homeworking to the image of homeworkers today. For example, in the mid-1970s, 82% of homeworkers who manufactured toys earned less than the statutory minimum rates in force at the time (ACAS, 1978: 45). A survey of wages in the clothing industry found eight times as many homeworkers as on-site workers with rates of pay below the minimum specified for the industry (Hakim and Dennis, 1982). Some surveys uncovered very low rates of pay indeed. For example, Brown (1974: 8–10) gave an example of a homeworker crocheting baby boots and another knitting Arran jumpers for just one-twentieth of the average hourly rate of pay for manual work at the time.

These findings were corroborated by other contemporaneous studies. These used a range of different methods, such as radio appeals (Brown, 1974), adverts in the printed media (Crine, 1979; Huws, 1984; Bisset and Huws, 1984), publicity campaigns (Yorkshire and Humberside Low Pay Unit, 1991), and doorstep surveys (Hope *et al.*, 1976; Allen and Wolkowitz, 1987; Felstead and Jewson, 1996, 1997). Similarly, even the National

Homeworking Survey of 1981 – an official survey carried out by the Department of Employment – found that almost seven out of ten (69%) of those working at home in manufacturing were lowly paid (Hakim, 1987: 106).

The survey evidence was also complemented by qualitative testimonies taken at the time. These outlined the difficulties homeworkers faced and the lack of alternative opportunities open to them. For example, a homeworker in Southwark interviewed in the mid-1980s said,

> When we say "homeworking" people imagine it is a woman's choice – that we want to work at home, under our own conditions and in our own comfort. But the real reason that most people fail to see is that *we have no choice other than to work at home* – especially as we often have young children and language problems. Therefore, homeworking is the other answer because we need the money badly.
>
> (quoted in Garrett, 1984: 1, original emphasis)

Others, such as this homeworker in Manchester, revealed what prompted them to take up homeworking and difficulties they faced in making ends meet,

> I am separating from my husband and I need extra cash. A friend told me about Christmas cracker making and put me in touch with the boss. He brings me the materials to me daily, and collects what I have done. He's always on to me to do more and more. At first, I was going to do just nights, but it now takes up all of my time. The materials mess up the whole house – lots of fiddly bits of paper. I have to make all the crackers, but the toys and jokes inside and pack in boxes, and cover with cellophane. If I work by myself I make 50p an hour, sometimes I get my children or a friend to help and I can make £1 an hour. Then at least I feel human because I can have a chat as well.
>
> (quoted in Greater Manchester Low Pay Unit, 1986: i)

This evidence prompted some organisations to call for greater regulation of the labour market to protect those involved. This culminated in the first attempt to give homeworkers the same legislative rights as other employees and give them greater protection. However, the *Homeworkers (Protection) Bill* of 1978 failed to gain sufficient support in Parliament. It also failed to do so on three further occasions in 1981, 1991, and 1996.

Throughout this period, there was a preoccupation with protecting the most vulnerable, typified by those working in manufacturing. Sometimes this was explicit as in the case of the Commission on Industrial Relations (the forerunner of the Advisory, Conciliation and Arbitration Service), which defined homeworkers as 'those who received work and payment directly from a manufacturing establishment and who did the work in their own homes' (CIR, 1973: 13). On other occasions, it was implicit with particular types of work excluded from the definition, hence focusing on a relatively narrow subset of employees who work at home. The definition used in the four unsuccessful *Homeworkers (Protection) Bills* is a good example of this approach. It defines a homeworker as

> an individual who contracts with a person not being a professional client of his (sic) for the purpose of that person's business, for the execution of any work (other than the production or creation of any literary, dramatic, artistic or musical work) to be done in domestic premises not under the control or management of the person with whom he (sic) contracts, and who does not normally make use of the services of more than two individuals in carrying out that work.

There are five distinct aspects to this definition that serve to exclude certain categories of individuals from its remit. As a result, it aims to isolate a group of individuals whose employment takes a particular form and are in need of protection. First, the work must be performed in domestic premises and not in premises owned and/or managed by the supplier of work. This excludes publicans who live on site, resident domestic servants, au pairs who live in the family household, and so on. It also excludes individuals who work from home rather than at home such as mini-cab drivers, plumbers, electricians, and insurance salespeople. These individuals use their home as a base from which to work with most of their work carried out away from the home. The activities they undertake include carrying people to and from destinations, fixing a leaking pipe, or rewiring a factory or house.

Secondly, the definition excludes individuals who act in a professional capacity such as tax consultants, chartered accountants, and solicitors. It also excludes a specific third category of work, namely those producing literary, dramatic, artistic, or musical work. Music arrangers, literary agents, authors, landscape artists, proof readers, and copy editors are therefore excluded. Both these exclusions are made on the grounds that people working at home in these occupations are either doing so on a self-employed basis or if they are employed they are less likely to need protection from low pay and other exploitative employment practices.

Fourthly, the definition includes people working for businesses or another person's business, but excludes those providing a service to another individual. This enables a distinction to be made between the sewing machinist who makes wedding dresses for her neighbours and friends for a fee, and the dressmaker who does the same job for a local clothing retailer. The definition only covers the second type of employment relationship since the former is likely to include entrepreneurs running small businesses. As a result, childminders are also excluded since they provide a personal service to another individual (the parent/guardian) but not for the 'purpose of that person's business'. In addition, those who do homework for more than one business are considered to have more than one homeworking job. Although they may enjoy more autonomy than those who work for a single supplier of work, they are defined as homeworkers by virtue of the fact that they are contracted by businesses to produce goods and services for eventual sale.

Fifthly, the definition excludes those who normally employ more than two people to carry out the work. This removes individuals who act as independent subcontractors and instead includes only those who, by and large, do the job themselves. In other words, homeworking 'agents' who farm out most of the work to others, but who do some of the work themselves, are excluded. Yet, irregular help, whether paid or unpaid, is insufficient to overturn the other 'homeworking' traits that individuals may possess.

This approach resists lumping together disparate groups of workers who have little in common with one another apart from the fact that they work at home. Previous studies have also adopted this approach (see Allen and Wolkowitz, 1987; Felstead and Jewson, 2000). Their focus is also on employees who work at home and are engaged in routine clerical activities (e.g. data entry or transcribing), repetitive manual tasks (e.g. packing boxes or stuffing envelopes), or manufacturing activities (e.g. making Christmas crackers or sewing garments). In other research, these are either referred to as manufacturing or industrial homeworkers (e.g. ILO, 2021). It is on these homeworkers that the debates of the 1970s, 1980s, and 1990s were primarily focused.

Even so, the debate was starting to shift as the economy was changing and new technologies were being developed. There was a shift away from a preoccupation with those working at home in manufacturing towards more of a focus on white-collar workers who could use technology to connect with their employer. At the time, these were often referred to as the 'new homeworkers', simply because the type of work undertaken was different (Huws, 1984). Most notably, it involved the use of information technology. This became the defining feature of what the literature refers to as 'teleworkers' (e.g. Huws, 1993; Sullivan, 2005).

However, it is not clear what role technology needs to play for the teleworking label to apply. Dependence on information technology varies and knowing where to draw the line is problematic. A web designer working at home, for example, may be wholly dependent on access to the Internet to do her work, while a sewing machinist may only pick up the telephone or send an email in order to arrange pick-up times for completed garments (Haddon and Brynin, 2005). Using technology as a defining feature of teleworking has become even more problematic. Since the 1980s and 1990s, remote communication devices have become commonplace and a part of everyday life. Indeed, their ubiquity has meant that more work has potentially become detached from place and carried out in a variety of places. This detachment is amply illustrated by the rise in the number of people able to work at home during the pandemic, enabled in no small part by the increasing connectivity we all enjoy (see Chapter 3). While the term teleworker signals the role played by technology in the decoupling of work from place, it has doubtful use as a distinctive social concept which adds value to those discussed throughout this chapter.

Nevertheless, the historical debates have left some indelible marks on the contemporary thinking. These include the importance of delineating those who work at home from one another, such as separating the self-employed – with or without employees – from those who are employed. Despite this, not all studies and authors always follow this basic principle. Research imperatives and pragmatism may, on occasion, require a different approach. Similarly, the experiences and circumstances of groups, such as employees who work at home, vary enormously. Some, for example, have loved the chance to work at home during the pandemic, while others could not wait to go back to the office. Either way, readers must be acutely aware of the meaning that different authors and studies attach to the same words since the same words can mean different things.

2.5 Conclusion

A key feature of 'homeworking' – as the word implies – is that the two worlds of home and work are carried out in the same spatial boundaries. The home simultaneously becomes a place where paid work is done, and a place where domestic relationships are played out and unpaid domestic labour is undertaken. However, as this chapter has shown, historical accounts of homeworking have focused on a much narrower group of workers, namely employees working in manufacturing and routine service work. These were typically among the most poorly paid and exploited members of the labour market. National and local campaigns sought to provide them with legislative protection and community support. As a result, the definitions used to frame the debate were intentionally narrow. However, contemporary debates, reports, and commentaries pay relatively little attention to delineating the social relations of production, apart from a focus on the location of where employees work and the consequences this might have for employers, employees, and society (as outlined in Chapters 4, 5, and 6). This needs to be borne in mind when interpreting the empirical findings reported in this book and elsewhere. That said, the instruction to work *at* home during the pandemic has meant that much of the research carried out during this time has, by definition, been focused on those who do not venture outside of the home but work within it.

Using the home as a base from which to work, on the other hand, weakens the extent to which these contrasting worlds overlap since those involved move from place to place to do their work. As such they are often referred to as 'mobile workers'. They include mobile hairdressers who visit other people's houses to cut clients' hair, carpet fitters who lay carpets in domestic and commercial premises, and local plumbers who fix and service domestic boilers (Cohen, 2010). Furthermore, these workers are often self-employed and as result they do not have an employer to whom they report through physical visits and/or communication devices.

However, 'remote work' refers to an aspect of the employer–employee relationship defined by situations 'where work, which could also be performed at the employer's premises, is *carried out away from those premises* on a regular basis' (Government of Ireland, 2021: 6, my emphasis). The Welsh Government defines remote working in similar terms as work 'which takes place *outside of a traditional office or "central" place of work.* It includes working at home and close to your local community' (Welsh Government, 2021, my emphasis).

Both these definitions define remote working as off-site working which is undertaken some or all of the time. Working at home, too, can be carried out on a full-time or part-time basis. As a result, some authors and commentators refer to this mixture of arrangements as 'hybrid working'. This term captures the idea that work can take place in a variety of places across the working week. However, at least some time is spent working on the employers' premises, typically the office. For hybrid workers, then, the office becomes the place from where some work is undertaken and to which workers remain connected, both physically and electronically (Halford, 2005). This is the working arrangement that many predict will become more prevalent in the years ahead (e.g. Bloom, 2021). These predictions are based on evidence that suggests that during the pandemic employees' appetite for working at home has grown and employers have got used to employees working off-site (see Chapter 6).

References

ACAS (1978) *Toy Manufacturing Wages Council*, Report, No. 13, London: Advisory, Conciliation and Arbitration Service.
Adams-Pressl, A, Boneva, T, Golin, M and Rauh, C (2020) *What Tasks Can Be Done From Home: Evidence on the Variation Within and Across Occupations and*

Industries, Cambridge Working Papers in Economics, No. 2020/23, Cambridge: University of Cambridge.

Allen, S and Wolkowitz, C (1987) *Homeworking: Myths and Realities*, London: Palgrave Macmillan.

Bain, P and Taylor, P (2000) 'Entrapped by the "electronic panopticon"? Worker resistance in the call centre', *New Technology, Work and Employment*, 15(1): 2–18.

Beavan-Seymour, C (2020a) *Labour Market Survey: Characteristics Report*, Newport: Office for National Statistics.

Beavan-Seymour, C (2020b) *Labour Market Survey: Technical Report*, Newport: Office for National Statistics.

Bisset, L and Huws, U (1984) *Sweated Labour: Homeworking in Britain Today*, London: Low Pay Unit.

Bloom, N (2021) *Hybrid Is the Future of Work*, Stanford Institute for Economic Policy Research (SIEPR) Policy Brief, Stanford: SIEPR, June.

Brown, M (1974) *Sweated Labour: A Study of Homework*, London: Low Pay Unit.

Burchell, B, Reuschke, D and Zhang, M (2021) 'Spatial and temporal segmenting of urban workplaces: the gendering of multi-locational working', *Urban Studies*, 58(11): 2207–2232.

Castells, M (2000) *The Rise of the Network Society*, Oxford: Blackwell.

Cohen, R I (2010) 'Rethinking "mobile work": boundaries of space, time and social relations in the working lives of mobile hairstylists', *Work, Employment and Society*, 24(1): 65–84.

Commission on Industrial Relations (1973) *Pin, Hook, and Eye and Snap Fastener Wages Council*, CIR Report, No. 49, London: HMSO.

Crang, P (1994) 'It's show time? On the workplace geographies of display in a restaurant in Southeast England', *Environment and Planning D: Society and Space*, 12: 675–704.

Crine, S (1979) *The Hidden Army*, London: Low Pay Unit.

Eurofound (2012) *Fifth European Working Conditions Survey*, Luxembourg: Publications of the European Union.

Eurofound (2020) *Living, Working and COVID-19*, Luxembourg: Publications of the European Union.

Fayard, A-L and Weeks, J (2007) 'Photocopiers and water-coolers: the affordances of informal interation', *Organization Studies*, 28(5): 605–634.

Felstead, A and Henseke, G (2017) 'Assessing the growth of remote working and its consequences for effort, well-being and work-life balance', *New Technology, Work and Employment*, 32(3): 195–212.

Felstead, A and Jewson, N (1995) 'Working at home: estimates from the 1991 census', *Employment Gazette*, 103(3): 95–99.

Felstead, A and Jewson, N (1996) *Homeworkers in Britain*, London: HMSO.

Felstead, A and Jewson, N (1997) 'Researching a problematic concept: homeworkers in Britain', *Work, Employment and Society*, 11(2): 327–346.

Felstead, A and Jewson, N (2000) *In Work, at Home: Towards an Understanding of Homeworking*, London: Routledge.

Felstead, A, Jewson, N, Phizacklea, A and Walters, S (2002) 'The option to work at home: another privilege for the favoured few?', *New Technology, Work and Employment*, 17(3): 188–207.

Felstead, A, Jewson, N and Walters, S (2005) *Changing Places of Work*, London: Palgrave.

Felstead, A and Reuschke, D (2021) 'A flash in the pan or a permanent change? The growth of homeworking during the pandemic and its effect on employee productivity in the UK', *Information Technology and People*, online first.

Foucault, M (1977) *Discipline and Punish*, Harmondsworth: Penguin, Peregrine Books.

Garrett, M (1984) *Homeworking in Southwark*, Report from the Southwark Employment Unit, London: Southwark Employment Unit.

Gottlieb, C, Grobovšek, J and Poschke, M (2020) 'Working from home across countries', *Covid Economics*, 8: 71–91.

Government of Ireland (2021) *Making Remote Work: National Remote Work Strategy*, Dublin: Department of Enterprise, Trade and Industry.

Greater Manchester Low Pay Unit (1986) *Homeworking in Manchester*, Economic Briefing Note, No. 62, Manchester: Manchester City Council.

Green, N (2002) 'On the move: technology, mobility and the mediation of social time and space', *The Information Society*, 18: 281–292.

Gronow, J and Warde, A (eds) (2001) *Ordinary Consumption*, London: Routledge.

Haddon, L and Brynin, M (2005) 'The character of telework and the characteristics of teleworkers', *New Technology, Work and Employment*, 20(1): 34–46.

Hakim, C (1987) *Home-Based Work in Britain: A Report on the 1981 National Homeworking Survey and the DE Research Programme on Homework*, Department of Employment Research Paper, No. 60. London: Department of Employment.

Hakim, C and Dennis, R (1982) *Homeworking in Wages Council Industries: A Study Based on Wages Inspectorate Records of Pay and Earnings*, Department of Employment Research Paper, No. 37, London: Department of Employment.

Halford, S (2005) 'Hybrid workspace: re-spatialisations of work, organisation and management', *New Technology, Work and Employment*, 20(1): 19–33.

Hensvik, L, Le Barbanchon, T and Roland, R (2020) *Which Jobs Are Done from Home? Evidence from the American Time Use Survey*, IZA Discussion Papers, No. 13138, Bonn: Institute of Labor Economics.

Hope, E, Kennedy, M and de Winter, A (1976) 'Homeworkers in North London', in Barker, D L and Allen, S (eds) *Dependence and Exploitation in Work and Marriage*, London: Longman.

Huws, U (1984) *The New Homeworkers: New Technology and the Changing Location of White-Collar Work*, Low Pay Unit Pamphlet, No. 28, London: Low Pay Unit.

Huws, U (1993) *Teleworking in Britain*, Employment Department Research Series, No. 18. London: Department of Employment.

ILO (2021) *Working from Home: From Invisibility to Decent Work*, Geneva: International Labour Office.

Laurier, E (2001a) 'The region as a socio-technical accomplishment of mobile workers', in Brown, B, Green, N and Harper, R (eds) *Wireless World: Social and Interactional Aspects of the Mobile Age*, London: Springer-Verlag.

Laurier, E (2001b) 'Why people say where they are during mobile phone calls', *Environment and Planning D: Society and Space*, 19: 485–504.

Laurier, E and Philo, C (1999) *"Meet You at Junction 17": A Socio-Technical and Spatial Study of the Mobile Office*, ESRC End of Award Report, R000222071, Swindon: ESRC.

Martin, J (2021) *Homeworking Hours, Rewards and Opportunities in the UK: 2011 to 2020*, Newport: Office for National Statistics.

Sullivan, C (2005) 'What's in a name? Definitions and conceptualisations of teleworking and homeworking', *New Technology, Work and Employment*, 18(3): 158–165.

Summerfield, P (1989) *Women Workers in the Second World War: Production and Patriarchy in Conflict*, London: Routledge.

Thompson, E P (1967) 'Time, work-discipline and industrial capitalism', *Past and Present*, 38: 56–97.

Thrift, N (1990) 'Owners' time and own time: the making of a capitalist time consciousness 1300–1800', in Hassard, J (ed) *The Sociology of Time*, London: Palgrave Macmillan.

Urry, J (2000) *Sociology Beyond Societies: Mobilities for the Twenty-First Century*, London: Routledge.

Welsh Government (2021) 'Remote working: how and why we want to promote remote working', https://gov.wales/remote-working (accessed 28 June 2021).

Wheatley, D (2017) 'Employee satisfaction and use of flexible working arrangements', *Work, Employment and Society*, 31(4): 567–585.

Yorkshire and Humberside Low Pay Unit (1991) *A Survey of Homeworking in Calderdale*, Batley: Yorkshire and Humberside Low Pay Unit.

3 Trends in Remote Working

'The only positive I can think of during this entire pandemic nightmare is that some of us may have learnt to read a graph', Gary Lineker, ex-footballer and TV presenter, on Twitter, 26 October 2020.

3.1 Introduction

For months during the pandemic, TV news bulletins on the BBC carried counts of the number of people newly infected with Covid-19, the number of people admitted to hospital with the disease, and, sadly, the number of deaths. These daily counts were displayed as a series of bar charts with lines added to represent the seven-day moving average. As the pandemic evolved, even more data were presented. The number of first and second dose vaccinations administered the previous day and the percentages of people in receipt of these doses were added to the lengthening list of charts and figures presented. Prime Ministerial briefings – which at the height of the pandemic took place daily – were also data heavy with the meaning of charts explained to millions of people. Many of those watching may not previously have known how, or had the inclination, to digest the meaning of figures displayed in a chart. However, the trajectory of the trends identified by these data has, in part, been used to determine when lockdowns were imposed and when restrictions were relaxed and lifted. It is no surprise, then, that the current presenter of *Match of the Day* suggests that many more of us have become accustomed to interpreting trends displayed in a graph or chart.

The aim of this chapter is to show – using visual devices such as the chart – that the move towards homeworking in the UK was happening well before the pandemic hit. Similar trends were also happening across the world. Moreover, homeworking was evolving away from manufacturing – typified by the sewing machinist and Christmas cracker maker – to include office workers who are, on average, much better paid than their

DOI: 10.4324/9781003247050-3

historical counterparts. However, this evolutionary change was turbo-charged by the pandemic as workers were told to work at home, whether they liked it or not (Anderson and Kelliher, 2020). This is evident not just in terms of the potentiality to detach work from the traditional office but also in terms of the actual number of people who have worked at home for months on end.

To achieve this aim, the chapter is split into three sections. The next section considers the period running up to the outbreak of the pandemic at the beginning of 2020 and the growing influence of technology in detaching work from place. This is followed by a section on the pre-pandemic potentiality of more and more work to be carried out away from employers' premises, at home, from home, or in a variety of places. This potentiality provided fertile ground for the explosion of homeworking during the pandemic witnessed in the UK, but also throughout the world. This evidence is discussed in the final substantive section of the chapter. This section also examines the changing characteristics of those involved and the jobs they do, and the implications these changes will have for the post-pandemic landscape.

3.2 Pre-pandemic Trends

Data on the location of work has been a feature of labour market surveys for a number of years. In a few cases, such data have been collected on a consistent basis over a number of decades. Even so, these data sometimes lack subtlety and do not always capture the fine-grain detail of everyday working life. Sometimes they focus on where people mainly work and therefore fail to capture the complexity of working patterns. On other occasions, they only present a limited number of possible work location options and therefore fail to capture places that are neither the home nor the premises of the employer. These 'third spaces' include cafés, restaurants, hotel lobbies, and even trains, buses, and planes used for business travel (Oldenberg, 2001). Furthermore, surveys typically use different questions with varying levels of precision, making comparisons difficult.

The longest running and consistent data series on the location of work in the UK is the Labour Force Survey (LFS). Most countries carry out similar exercises (e.g. Mehdi and Morisette, 2021). In the UK, each LFS contains data on a random sample of around 45,000 workers aged 16 and above. In 1981, the LFS included its first question on the location of work. Respondents were asked 'do you work mainly' in one of four locations: in your own home, in the same buildings or grounds as your home, in different places using home as a base, or somewhere quite different from home. The same question was posed again in 1992 and has been asked quarterly ever since (see Chapter 2 and Table 2.1).

Stacking results from each LFS alongside others in the series provides an insight into changes over time. Given the frequency with which questions on the location of work are asked, the analysis for this chapter is based on surveys stretching from 1981 to 2019. However, some of the analyses reported here are restricted to shorter time periods, given data availability.

These results suggest that, before the pandemic, the majority of people carried out their work somewhere separate from where they live; that is, in conventional locations such as shops, offices, and factories. However, this proportion was falling over time. Homeworking, on the other hand, was on a gradual, but slow, upward trajectory. In the year immediately before the pandemic, one in 20 (4.7%) of those employed worked mainly at home, double the proportion reporting that they worked mainly at home in 2003 and triple the proportion in 1981 (1.5%). The proportion using their home as a base from which to work was also on the up. In 2019, 8.4% of workers (one in 12) carried out their work in a variety of places using their home as a base, up from just 2.8% in 1981. Taking these two pieces of evidence together, in 1981, 4.3% of employed people in the UK worked mainly at or from their own home. Almost 40 years later, this proportion had risen to 12.9%, representing 4.2 million workers, or quadruple the number recorded in 1981 (see Figure 3.1).

Figure 3.1 Pre-pandemic Trends in the Use of the Home as a Place of Work, UK, 1981–2019

Source: Own calculations, updating Felstead, 2012.

Note: The data are based on the annual LFS in 1981 and the spring/second quarter LFS in 1992–2019.

A further question was added in 1997 which identified those who worked at least one full day in these locations. However, this question was asked of a restricted sample in surveys carried out between 2015 and 2019 (see Table 2.1). Using these data, then, we can identify people who worked at home occasionally rather than permanently between 1997 and 2014. This includes, for example, someone who spent four days a week working in an office, but one day working at home (cf. Haddad *et al.*, 2008). Periods of less than a full day, however, are not included in the count. Nor does the count include those who worked at home several hours a day, even if when totted up this equates to a full day's work. As a result, the estimates produced are conservative. Nevertheless, they suggest that around one in five (19.0%) workers in the UK used their home to some extent as their place of work in 2014. This equates to 5.8 million people.

The pre-pandemic data also reveal that the growth in the use of the home as a base from which to work had started to plateau. Those reporting that they mainly worked in this way grew up until 2003, but then it hovered at 8–9%. Furthermore, those working one day a week from home barely moved throughout this period and accounted for less than 1% of those in work. Those reporting that they worked mainly at home, on the other hand, have been on the rise for the last two decades (cf. Figure 3.1). Those working at home for one day a week have also been on the up – rising from 4.0% in 1997 to 5.9% in 2014 when the last available data were collected. On this evidence, the growth in mobile working was faltering well before the pandemic hit, while homeworking – as the main place of work or a part-time basis – was becoming more prevalent year on year.

Other sources of evidence also suggest that, even before the pandemic, the single workplace was weakening its grip on the concept of being 'in work'. According to the 2011 Census, for example, almost a fifth (18.5%) of those in employment aged 16–74 years old had no fixed place to report or else they worked at or from home. This amounts to 4.9 million people. However, these data are not based on direct reports of work location as in the case of many of the surveys discussed in this book. Instead, they are derived from the individual's workplace address with 'no fixed place' given as an option. Those specifying a place of work were asked how they travelled to that address. The list of options includes car, train, on foot and, since 2001 'works mainly at or from home'.

A further source of evidence is the Skills and Employment Survey series, which focuses on the skills workers use at work and the quality of their working lives (Felstead and Henseke, 2017; Felstead *et al.*, 2015, 2019). Work location data were collected in the 2001, 2006, 2012, and 2017 surveys, which collected data from 4,470, 7,787, 3,200, and 3,306 workers, respectively. The question was designed to capture respondents' main location of work. The response options given differ from those used by the LFS which are steeped in a tradition that sees a clear divide between home and work, with little in between. LFS data relating to working at or from home do not allow us to assess the extent to which the conventional work-place is itself being used differently – possibly as a base from which to visit clients or as a drop-in centre. Nor does it capture the full extent to which people are working while in transit. The SES options, therefore, include working in a variety of places (using either home or the office as a base) and working on the move. Neither of these options is fully captured by the LFS.

The results corroborate the conclusion that the conventional workplace was not the main place of work for a sizeable minority of workers in Brit-ain well before the pandemic began. More than a third of workers reported that their job did not require them to spend most of their time working in 'a single workplace away from home (e.g. office, factory, or shop)'. Further-more, the proportion working in these conventional workplaces fell from 74.5% to 63.1% between 2001 and 2017. The use of unconventional loca-tions, on the other hand, rose. So, by 2017, a fifth (20.9%) of workers were mainly working in a variety of places, up four percentage points from 2001. There were also rises among those working at home and in the vicinity of the home (see Table 3.1). Some research suggests that these estimates may understate the extent of the shift. For example, based on the EWCS 2015, Burchell *et al.* (2021) estimate that across the EU 30% of women and 54% of men are in jobs that did not require them to attend the premises of their employer.

Technology has played an important role in this process, although it should not be used as a defining characteristic of working off-premises. After all, technology has transformed the working lives of many. Indeed, it is difficult to contemplate life without the devices and connectivity we now take for granted (Mullan and Wacjman, 2019). For example, the Skills and Employment Survey shows that using a computer was regarded as an essential part of over half (52.5%) of all jobs, up from three out of ten jobs (30.5%) in 1997. At the other end of the scale, only one in ten jobs (10.6%) did not require the use of a computer in 2017, down from 30.3% in 1997.

Nevertheless, some of the conditions for the explosion of homework-ing during the pandemic were in place well before lockdowns and restric-tions were imposed and workers were told to work at home if possible. The proportion of households with internet access, for example, has grown rapidly – up from around 9% in 1998 to 96% in 2020 (ONS, 2020a). At the same time, devices and applications as well as broadband speeds and cov-erage have revolutionised everyday life. It is hard to believe, for example, that the iPhone – the first smartphone to combine a computer, a digital cam-era, and a mobile phone into a single device – was launched in 2007. The

Table 3.1 Location of Work: Skills and Employment Survey Estimates, Britain, 2001–2017

Main Work Location	2001 (%)	2006 (%)	2012 (%)	2017 (%)
At home	2.9	3.6	4.4	5.2
In same grounds and buildings as home (e.g. adjoining property or land)	1.3	2.0	4.6	6.6
In a single workplace away from home (e.g. office, factory, or shop)	74.8	72.0	66.4	63.1
In a variety of different places of work (e.g. working on clients' premises or in their homes)	17.0	17.5	20.4	20.9
Working on the move (e.g. delivering products or people to different places)	4.1	5.0	4.2	4.3

Source: Own calculations, updating Felstead and Henseke, 2017.

ability to make video calls on the iPhone was added three years later. Holding video conferences with multiple callers on a laptop, smartphone, or tablet is a more recent innovation. Zoom was launched in April 2011, Google Meet in February 2017, and Teams was unveiled a month later that year.

Technology was therefore detaching work from place well before the pandemic began. This can be seen in some of the pre-pandemic evidence. For example, since 1997, respondents to the spring (now second calendar quarter) LFS have been asked whether they use a computer *and* a telephone to work at or from home. If so, they were asked whether these tools were essential for them to work in this way. This shows a steady rise in the importance of the computer and the telephone for those working at or from home (see Figure 3.2). The proportion of such workers who were reliant on these devices rose from around a third in 1997 to four-fifths in 2019, the year before the pandemic began. On the basis of this evidence, many researchers agree that while technology is a facilitator of, and an enabler for, homeworking, this does not mean that the growth of homeworking is inevitable (Boys, 2020; Bela *et al.*, 2020). Furthermore, connectivity across the UK is improving year on year, but broadband speeds remain low in some rural areas and are non-existent in others. Nevertheless, the potentiality for more work to be done at home is on the up and was in place well before the pandemic began. In fact, there is evidence to suggest that the upsurge in homeworking may be driving the development of future technologies. For example, an analysis of patent applications in the US shows that applications which mentioned terms related to this way of working – such as remote

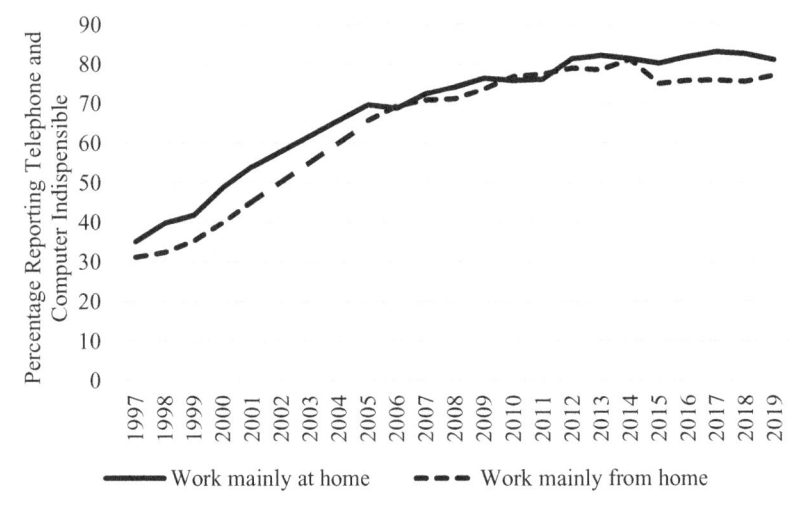

Figure 3.2 Computer and Telephone Indispensable to Working at/From Home, UK, 1997–2019

Source: Own calculations, Labour Force Survey, spring/second quarter 1997–2019.

working, nomadic working, teleworking, and home-based working – more than doubled in 2020 compared to the annual average for each of years between 2010 and 2019 (Bloom *et al.*, 2021). These new innovations may make it even easier to work outside of the office in the future.

3.3 Hidden Potential

In a bid to arrest the spread of Covid-19, governments across the world introduced social distancing restrictions and advised employers to allow their workers to work at home if they can. Periodic national lockdowns served to limit movement even further with advice to work at home turning into an instruction to do so. In the light of these changes, researchers began to investigate how many and what type of jobs could potentially be done at home. The estimates produced and the pictures presented are based on data collected before the pandemic. Furthermore, they are based on what might be possible and not on where people actually work. They therefore reveal the hidden potential of working at home.

The first to produce such evidence were Dingel and Neiman (2020). They developed an algorithm based on answers given to surveys about jobs in the US. In particular, they drew on two Occupational Information Network (O*NET) surveys (Tippin and Hilton, 2010). The first is focused on the work context. It consists of 57 questions about the work setting, the hazards involved, the pace of work, and the extent to which the work involves dealing with other people. Respondents were asked to report the frequency of certain situations arising or the amount of time they spend doing things as part of the job. The second survey is focused on the work activities undertaken. It consists of 84 questions about a range of tasks that may or may not be part of the job. Respondents were asked to rate the importance of certain activities on 1–5 scale, ranging from not important to essential. O*NET collects these data from workers in almost 1,000 occupations and has been doing so since 1998. Every year updates to the database are made with new versions published. Data for each occupation are based on responses from an average of 26 respondents in the case of the work context survey and 25 respondents in the case of the work activities survey (www.onetcenter.org/).

Dingel and Neiman (2020) pick out 15 questions from these two surveys and use the responses given to categorise jobs into two groups – those that can be done at home and those that cannot. Certain conditions have to be met for jobs to be considered appropriate for homeworking. These include the frequency with which email was used, the importance of outdoor work, the frequency of face-to-face interaction, the use of electrical and mechanical equipment, and exposure to hazards. Jobs are classified as *inappropriate* for homeworking if, on average, those in the occupational group reported, for example, using email less than once a month or that working directly with the public is very or extremely important.

Seven of the conditions are taken from the work context survey. If respondents, on average, reported that any of the following apply, then the occupation is coded as one which *cannot* be done at home:

- using email less than once a month;
- dealing with violent people at least once a week;
- being exposed to diseases or infection at least once a week;
- being exposed to minor burns, cuts, bites, or stings at least once a week;
- spending the majority of their work time walking or running;
- spending the majority of their work time wearing protective clothing or using safety equipment; and
- a majority of respondents reported working outdoors every day.

Eight of the conditions are taken from the work activity survey. Once again, if any of these conditions apply, the occupational group is deemed inappropriate for homeworking. These conditions apply if respondents reported that any of the following activities was very or extremely important for the job:

- performing general physical activities;
- handling and moving objects;
- controlling machines and processes [not including computers or vehicles];
- operating vehicles, mechanical devices, or equipment;
- performing for or working directly with the public;
- repairing and maintaining mechanical equipment;
- repairing and maintaining electronic equipment; and
- inspecting equipment, structures, or materials.

The resulting algorithm is then applied to US-level occupational data held by the US Bureau of Labor Statistics (BLS). This suggests that up to 37% of US jobs could be done at home. However, this figure varies considerably by broad occupational group. Farmers, construction workers, and production operatives, for example, have virtually no chance of being able to work at home according to the algorithm. On the other hand, working at home is possible for managers, educators, and those working in computing, finance, and law. Not surprisingly, therefore, the data also reveal that the ability to work at home rises steadily with pay; that is, it is higher among the better paid and lower among the poorer paid (Dingel and Neiman, 2020: Table 1 and Figure 1).

Subsequent research has taken one of two paths. Either researchers have applied the algorithm lock, stock, and barrel to a different country or they have made amendments to it. Examples of the former include Rodríguez (2020) for Wales and Deng *et al.* (2020) for Canada. Both use the international classification system of occupations developed by the International Labour Organisation (ILO) as a crosswalk between the system used in the US and in their own country. This therefore allows the US classification of homeworking occupations to be translated into another country's context. On this basis, it is estimated that 39.9% of jobs in Wales and 45.2% of jobs across the UK could be done at home, while in Canada the equivalent figure is 38.9% (Rodríguez, 2020; Deng *et al.*, 2020). A range of other estimates have been produced for other countries which put the potentiality between a quarter and a third of jobs (ILO, 2020).

Another approach is to make amendments to the algorithm. The ONS in the UK, for example, focuses on survey questions of its own choosing, some of which are different from those chosen by the US authors (ONS, 2020b). These are grouped into five categories: the extent to which the job has to be carried out in a specific location; the amount of face-to-face interaction with others; the frequency of exposure to burns, infections, and other hazards; the extent to which the job requires physical activity; and to what extent tools and/or protective equipment are required. In addition, instead of using these data to create a binary divide, the ONS approach uses the granularity of the data to produce a more complex picture. It therefore puts occupations along a likelihood continuum of being able to be done at home; it does not provide an estimate of the number of jobs that could be carried out at home in their entirety. Instead, the data provide users with an interactive tool with which to assess the likelihood jobs can be done at home. Users can choose jobs from a drop-down list of 369 job titles (ONS, 2020b).

Despite this slightly different approach, the ONS results also suggest that employees who earn higher hourly wages are more likely to be able to work at home. For example, chief executives and senior officials – whose median earnings are £44.08 an hour – are among those most able to work at home, as are financial managers and directors (£31.38) and programmers and software development professionals (£21.97). On the other hand, gardeners – whose median hourly earnings are £10.27 – are very unlikely to be able to work at home, as are carpenters and joiners (£13.18) and elementary construction occupations, such as labourers (£10.25).

It is useful at this point to reflect on these empirical studies in the light of the conceptual issues raised in Chapter 2. The first point relates to whether the jobs identified are jobs that can *only* be done at home or whether they are jobs that can be done in a variety of places, including the home. Closer inspection of the O*NET questions used by Dingel and Neiman (2020) suggests the latter. They seek to identify jobs that require an employer-controlled environment (such as a factory or office) that can minimise hazards from people and/or machines, or jobs which require engagement with objects, equipment, and/or the public (such as in a shop or warehouse). This approach identifies jobs that need to be carried out in a traditional workplace. By definition, this means that those falling outside this group can be carried out in a variety of places, including the home, the local café, community centre, or even on the move. The ONS approach does much the same; it identifies the extent to which jobs are location-specific. This means that aspects of a job that are not dependent on a particular location can, potentially at least, be undertaken in a variety of places with working at home being one of a number of options. The jobs identified can therefore be done remotely to varying degrees rather than at home only.

Secondly, the questions selected to make the classification preclude the possibility that certain types of work can be done at home. This flies in the face of the historical evidence which suggests that manufacturing has been carried out at home for centuries. Clothing workers such as sewing machinists and overlockers as well as assemblers of Christmas crackers, handbags, nappies, and children's toys, for example, regularly use mechanised devices and equipment to carry out their work at home. However, the questions used by Dingel and Neiman (2020) suggest that such devices and equipment cannot be located in the home. This drawback is particularly pronounced when the approach is applied to poorer countries across the world where manufacturing homeworking is more common (Gottlieb *et al.*, 2020; ILO, 2021). In India, for example, it is estimated that there are 37 million such workers, mostly women working as beedi rollers (leaf-rolled cigarettes made out of coarse and uncured tobacco) or embroiderers for the country's garment industry (Mazumdar, 2018).

Thirdly, the location of work is more complex than implied by the Dingel and Neiman (2020) approach. For them, there is a binary divide between jobs that can be done at home and those that cannot. The world of work is not that clear-cut as reflected in the ONS (2020b) continuum approach. This suggests the time spent working in particular places may vary and that working at home is not an 'all or nothing' concept. The notion of hybrid working acknowledges this complexity.

Instead of using survey questions about the nature of the work undertaken and then making assumptions about whether this activity could or could not be carried out a home, an alternative approach is to directly ask workers what proportion of tasks could be done at home. This tactic was adopted in two surveys carried out in the UK and the US in early March and early April 2020. Around 4,000 workers took part in each of these surveys (Adams-Pressl *et al.*, 2020). On average, workers in the UK surveys reported being able to do 43% of their tasks at home (the figure for the US was slightly higher at 45%). The results also show that while there were spikes in the proportion reporting being able to do none or all of their work tasks at home, most workers fell somewhere in-between. This variation is repeated within the same occupation and industry groups. These results, then, suggest that many workers could work some of the time in the office and some of the time at home (or elsewhere). They also suggest that the balance between the two can vary substantially, even within a similar group of jobs. However, unlike the research reported so far, these research results suggest that there is a U-shaped relationship between income and the proportion of tasks that can be done at home. That is, workers with very low incomes report being able to do a fairly large share of their tasks at home, but the proportion falls as income rises before rising steadily again to reach a peak among high earners.

3.4 Explosion of Working at Home

The technological infrastructure for an increase in homeworking was in place well before the pandemic began (see Figure 3.2). Furthermore, the potential for more work tasks to be carried out at home, if needed, was also in place. It should therefore come as little surprise that the explosion of homeworking in response to the pandemic was possible. Nevertheless, the scale of the change was dramatic.

The outbreak of Covid-19 marked a sudden change – the evolution in work location gave way to a full-blooded revolution. Homeworking rocketed as a result of the advice to work at home and the introduction of a series of lockdowns between March 2020 and March 2021. Evidence from the Understanding Society Covid-19 Survey suggests that the proportion reporting that they worked exclusively at home in the UK rose from 5.7% immediately before these restrictions and lockdowns were introduced to 43.1% in April 2020 and fell as lockdowns were lifted, reaching 23.5% in September 2020. However, they began to rise again as lockdowns were reintroduced at the turn of the year, peaking at 37.0% in January 2021 before falling back a little two months later (see Figure 3.3). In numerical

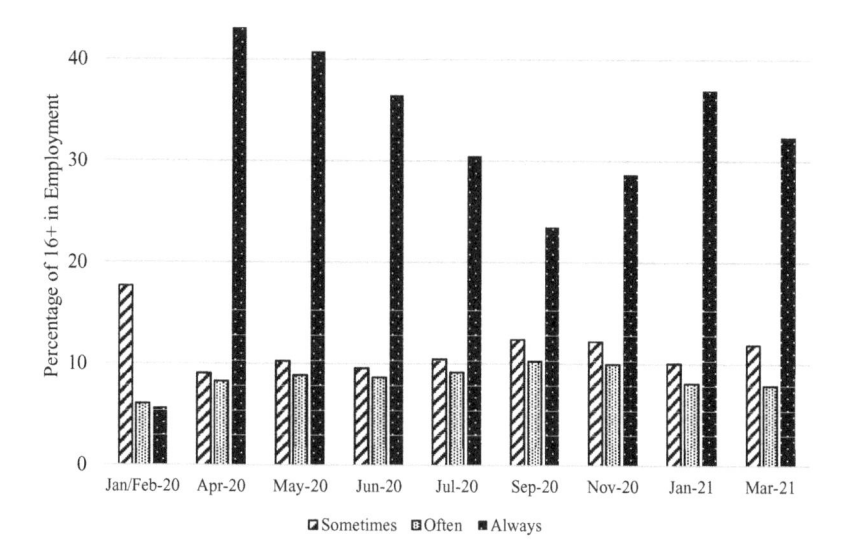

Figure 3.3 Prevalence of Homeworking in the UK, January/February 2020–March 2021

Source: Own calculations from the Understanding Society Covid-19 Study, April 2020– March 2021.

terms, the number of full-time homeworkers rose from 1.8 million before the pandemic to 12.5 million in April 2020. This number is estimated to have fallen subsequently, but to have remained at around 8 million for much of the pandemic (Felstead, 2021: Table A3).

Other surveys reveal the same pattern with homeworking remaining high in line with UK Government guidance to work at home possible. Figure 3.4 is based on data taken from the ONS's Opinions and Lifestyle Survey. This is a survey of around 2,500 working adults which has been carried out on an almost weekly basis since March 2020 (ONS, 2021b). The results suggest that throughout the early months of the pandemic between 40–50% of workers were carrying out work at home. However, the proportion fell to around one in four workers in late August 2020 as restrictions were lifted and there were calls for office workers to return to work. However, the proportion working at home rose again, as lockdowns were reintroduced and restrictions tightened. This meant that the proportion working at home (43%) because of coronavirus in mid-February 2021 was similar to the level in April 2020. Since that time, the proportion fell, but even in late August 2021, it was very high by historical standards (cf. Figure 3.1).

International evidence, too, suggests an explosion in working at home. To capture the immediate economic and social effects of the pandemic,

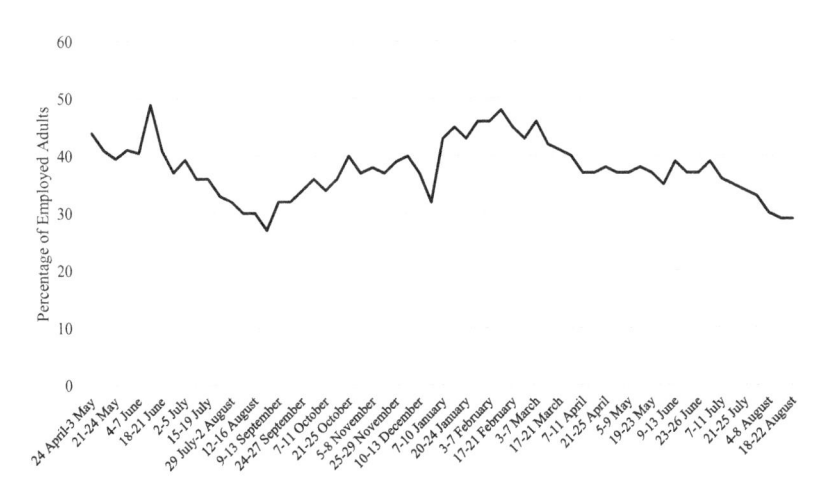

Figure 3.4 Prevalence of Working at Home Because of Covid-19, UK, March 2020–August 2021

Source: Data taken from the Opinions and Lifestyle Survey (ONS, 2021a).

Eurofound launched a large-scale online survey across the European Union in April 2020. Within three months or so, 87,000 people had taken part. While participation in the survey was by self-selection, weights can be applied to make the survey results broadly representative of the demographic profile of member states (Eurofound, 2020a, 2020b). According to this evidence, over a third of respondents across the EU were working at home because of the pandemic. But the proportion varied widely, from over half in Finland, Luxembourg, Belgium, and the Netherlands to less than a quarter in Slovenia and Romania (see Figure 3.5).

Elsewhere across the developed world, similar spikes in working at home have been recorded.

- Based on commuting data, Bick *et al.* (2021) report that 35.2% of the workforce in the US worked entirely at home in May 2020, up from 8.2% in February 2020. In addition, 28.6% of those continuing to travel to work said that they worked at home some of the time.
- Working at home also spiked in Canada; only 4% reported working most of their hours at home in 2016, but by the beginning of 2021 this had risen to 32% (Mehdi and Morisette, 2021).
- Job holders in Australia were also more likely to report working at home one or more times a week in February 2021 (41%) compared to March 2020 (24%) when Covid-19 restrictions were first introduced (Australian Bureau of Statistics, 2021).

A common feature of the sharp rise in homeworking during the pandemic, both in the UK and elsewhere, is that its growth has not been evenly spread. The largest surges were recorded among the most privileged segments of the UK labour market – the better educated, the higher skilled, and the higher paid. For example, according to data from the Understanding Society Covid-19 Study, the proportion of graduates reporting that they worked exclusively at home rose from 8.0% before the pandemic to 59.2% during the pandemic (defined here as the months of April, May, and June 2020). On the other hand, the growth in homeworking among those with no qualifications was more muted despite starting from a relatively low base. It rose by just five percentage points as a result of the pandemic with the vast majority (84.0%) of lowly qualified workers working outside the home (see Figure 3.6a).

Similarly, while homeworking grew across all occupational groups during the first three months of the pandemic, it grew particularly rapidly among higher skilled occupational groups. For example, during this period, a majority of those working as managers, professionals, associate professionals (e.g. computer assistants, buyers, and estate agents), and administrative

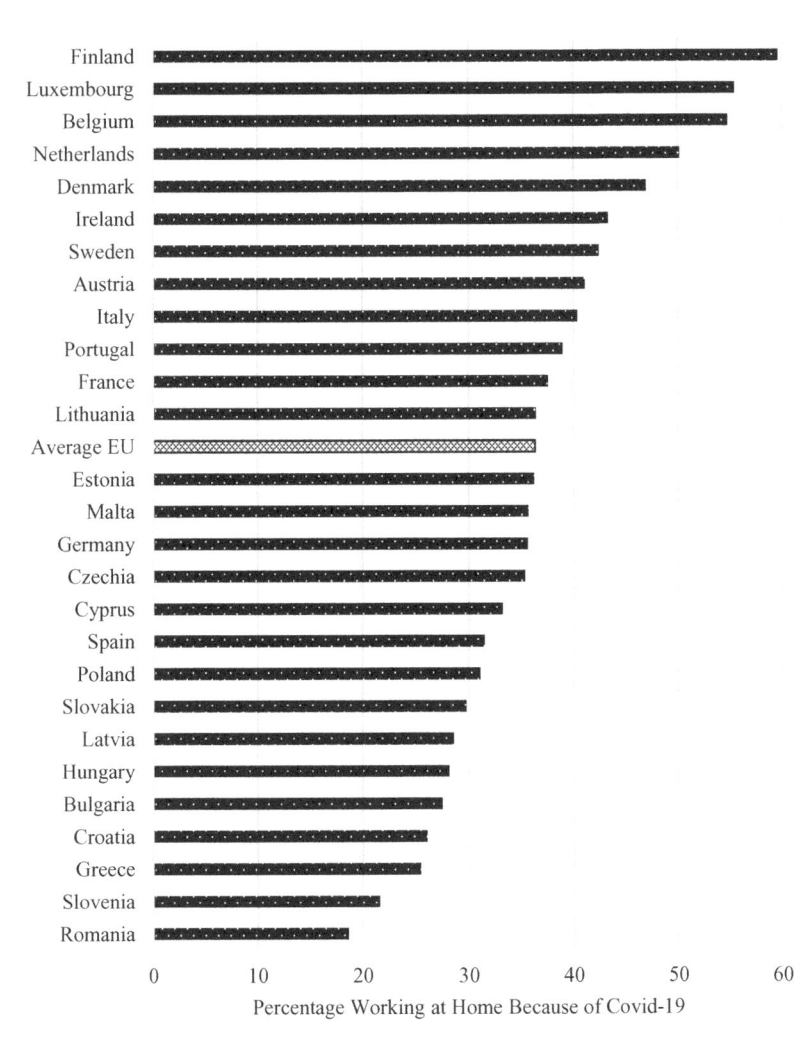

Figure 3.5 Growth of Working at Home as a Result of Covid-19 Across the European Union

Source: Own calculations from Eurofound data, but similar also produced in Eurofound (2020a, 2020b: Figure 7).

Note: Respondents were asked, 'Have you started to work from home as a result of the Covid-19 situation?'

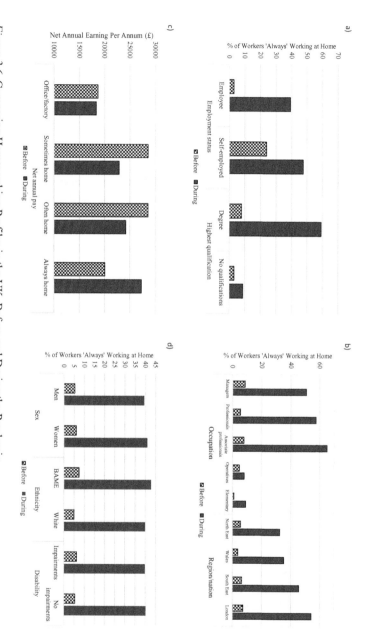

Figure 3.6 Comparing Homeworking Profiles in the UK, Before and During the Pandemic

Source: Felstead, 2021.

Note: 'During the pandemic' is defined as the months of April, May, and June 2020.

and secretarial staff (e.g. personal assistants, office clerks, and bookkeepers) reported that they did all of their work at home. This was up from 5–9% before the pandemic. However, workers operating in lower skilled occupations continued to use the factory, shop, or office as their workplace both before and during the pandemic. For example, more than four out of five operatives and elementary workers (e.g. machine operators, assemblers, and labourers) reported that none of their work was carried out at home (see Figure 3.6b). Yet these were the types of jobs on which homeworking research in 1970s, 1980s, and 1990s was primarily focused (cf. section 2.4).

The pay profile of homeworkers also changed with the net annual pay of workers who did all of their work at home rising from around £20,000 before the pandemic began to around £27,250 during the first three months of restrictions. On the other hand, the pay profile of those who worked at home often or sometimes fell, while the pay profile of those who worked outside of the home declined slightly. This suggests that the shift towards homeworking was strongest among the higher paid (see Figure 3.6c).

Certain industries and regions also saw dramatic rises in the prevalence of homeworking. For example, during the first three months of the pandemic approaching, two-thirds of those working in banking and finance (63.0%), over a half of those based in London (54.3%) and approaching a half of those based in the South East (45.5%) reported that they did all of their work at home. These proportions were up from around 7% before the pandemic began (see Figure 3.6b).

However, the growth of homeworking was fairly evenly spread among workers with different personal demographic profiles. For example, the growth in the proportions exclusively working at home rose at a similar rate among Black, Asian, and Minority Ethnic (BAME) workers as it did among others. The same goes for disability and gender (see Figure 3.6d). The only exception is age where the growth of homeworking was more pronounced among younger workers.

This picture is repeated internationally with the spike in homeworking most pronounced among: managerial, professional, and related occupations; geographical areas with a higher share of these occupations; and individuals who possess higher qualifications and receive better pay (e.g. Brynjolfsson *et al.*, 2020; Bick *et al.*, 2020). Moreover, many of these patterns are statistically significant in multivariate models which take into account these bivariate differences (Barrero *et al.*, 2021).

3.5 Conclusion

Even before the pandemic, the location of work was changing, albeit gradually. There was a slow but steady rise in homeworking. In the UK, it was relatively rare in 1981 when only 1.5% of those in employment reported working mainly at home, but by 2019 it had tripled to 4.7%. Similar trends were evident elsewhere. In the US, for example, the proportion of employees who primarily worked from home grew from less than 1% in 1980 to 2.4% in 2010 and 4.0% in 2018 (Mateyka *et al.*, 2012; Barrero *et al.*, 2021).

However, the potential to work at home was growing even more rapidly. Mobile communication technology was increasingly detaching work from place. The smartphone, better internet quality, and video conferencing were making it easier and easier for office workers to be 'in work, at home'. Estimates based on pre-pandemic evidence suggest that almost half of all UK jobs could, if necessary, be done at home. It is hardly surprising, then, that around the same proportion of jobs were actually carried out at home when – in order to limit the spread of coronavirus – the UK Government told workers to do just that. The pre-pandemic evolutionary trend towards homeworking was, therefore, replaced by a full-blooded revolution.

It was significant in conceptual terms, too, since it meant that paid work was being done in the private sphere of the home where childcare, cooking, and cleaning were also carried out. Such workers experienced the full force of the conflicting pressures of the world of work and home since they were working *at* home. As a consequence, they and their fellow household members had to manage, reconcile, and accommodate these conflicting pressures (see Chapter 5).

What the patterns also demonstrate is a change in the nature of the 'homeworking' labour force. A movement away from jobs in manufacturing – which are low skilled, poorly paid, and are done by women and migrant labour – to 'office jobs' – which are better paid, more skilled, and are carried out by higher qualified men and women drawn from all parts of society. This shift had been underway for many years, but the pandemic changed the character of homeworking beyond recognition. The literature over the last half a century needs to be read with this dramatic shift in mind. Today's homeworker is no longer typified by the Christmas cracker maker or sewing machinist but is more likely to be the finance director or personal assistant. As subsequent chapters will go on to outline, this has significant implications for the future of office work, the buildings in which such work has traditionally been undertaken, and how office workers are managed.

References

Adams-Pressl, A, Boneva, T, Golin, M and Rauh, C (2020) *What Tasks Can Be Done from Home: Evidence on the Variation Within and Across Occupations and Industries*, Cambridge Working Papers in Economics, No. 2020/23, Cambridge: University of Cambridge.

Anderson, D and Kelliher, C (2020) 'Enforced remote working and the work-life interface during lockdown', *Gender in Management: An International Journal*, 35(7–8): 677–683.

Australian Bureau of Statistics (2021) *Household Impacts of COVID-19 Survey*, Canberra: Australian Bureau of Statistics.

Barrero, J M, Bloom, N and Davis, S J (2021) *Why Working from Home Will Stick*, NBER Working Paper Series, Working Paper, No. 28731, Cambridge, MA: National Bureau of Economic Research.

Bela, A F, Wilkinson, D and Monahan, E (2020) *Technology Intensity and Home-working in the UK*, Newport: Office for National Statistics.

Bick, A, Blandin, A and Mertens, K (2020) 'Work from home after the COVID-19 outbreak', *Federal Bank of Dallas Working Paper 2017*, Dallas: Federal Bank of Dallas.

Bick, A, Blandin, A and Mertens, K (2021) *Work from Home Before and After the COVID-19 Outbreak*, Federal Reserve Bank of Dallas Working Paper, No. 2017, Dallas: Federal Reserve Bank of Dallas (revised February 2021).

Bloom, N, Davies, S J and Zhestkova, Z (2021) *COVID-19 Shifted Patent Applications Toward Technologies That Support Working from Home*, Becker Friedman Institute Working Paper, No. 123, Chicago: Becker Friedman Institute.

Boys, J (2020) *Working from Home: What's Driving the Rise in Remote Working?*, London: Chartered Institute of Personnel and Development.

Brynjolfsson, E, Horton, J, Ozimek, A, Rock, D, Sharma, G and TuYe, H-Y (2020) *Covid-19 and Remote Work: An Early Look at US Data*, NBER Working Paper Series, Working Paper, No. 27344, Cambridge, MA: National Bureau of Economic Research.

Burchell, B, Reuschke, D and Zhang, M (2021) 'Spatial and temporal segmenting of urban workplaces: the gendering of multi-locational working', *Urban Studies*, 58(11): 2207–2232.

Deng, Z, Morissette, R and Messacar, D (2020) *Running the Economy Remotely: Potential for Working from Home During and After COVID-19*, Ottawa: Statistics Canada.

Dingel, J and Neiman, B (2020) *How Many Jobs Can Be Done at Home?*, NBER Working Paper Series, Working Paper, No. 26948, Cambridge, MA: National Bureau of Economic Research.

Eurofound (2020a) *Living, Working and COVID-19 Dataset*, Dublin: European Foundation for the Improvement of Living and Working Conditions.

Eurofound (2020b) *Living, Working and COVID-19*, Luxembourg: Publications of the European Union.

Felstead, A (2012) 'Rapid change or slow evolution? Changing places of work and their consequences in the UK', *Journal of Transport Geography*, 21(2): 31–38.

Felstead, A (2021) *Outlining the Contours of the "Great Homeworking Experiment" and Its Implications for Wales*, Senedd Economy, Infrastructure and Skills Committee Commissioned Report, Cardiff: Senedd Cymru.

Felstead, A, Gallie, D and Green, F (2015) *Unequal Britain at Work*, Oxford: Oxford University Press.

Felstead, A, Gallie, D, Green, F and Henseke, G (2019) 'Conceiving, designing and trailing a short form measure of job quality: a proof-of-concept study', *Industrial Relations Journal*, 50(1): 2–19.

Felstead, A and Henseke, G (2017) 'Assessing the growth of remote working and its consequences for effort, well-being and work-life balance', *New Technology, Work and Employment*, 32(3): 195–212.

Gottlieb, C, Grobovšek, J and Poschke, M (2020) 'Working from home across countries', *Covid Economics*, 8: 71–91.

Haddad, H, Lyons, G and Chatterjee, K (2008) 'An examination of determinants influencing the desire for and frequency of part-day and whole-day homeworking', *Journal of Transport Geography*, 17(2): 124–133.

ILO (2020) *Working from Home: Estimating the Worldwide Potential*, ILO Brief, Geneva: International Labour Office, April.

ILO (2021) *Working from Home: From Invisibility to Decent Work*, Geneva: International Labour Office.

Mateyka, P J, Rapino, M and Landivar, L C (2012) *Home-Based Workers in the United States: 2010*, US Census Bureau, Current Population Reports, Washington, DC: US Census Bureau.

Mazumdar, I (2018) *Home-Based Work in 21st Century India*, Occasional Paper, No. 64, New Delhi: Centre for Women's Development Studies.

Mehdi, T and Morisette, R (2021) *Working from Home: Productivity and Preferences*, Ottawa: Statistics Canada.

Mullan, K and Wacjman, J (2019) 'Have mobile devices changed working patterns in the 21st century? A time-diary analysis of work extension in the UK', *Work, Employment and Society*, 33(1): 3–20.

Oldenberg, R (2001) *Celebrating the Third Place: Inspiring Stories About the "Great Good Places" at the Heart of Our Communities*, New York: Marlowe.

ONS (2020a) *Internet Access – Households and Individuals, Great Britain: 2020*, Newport: Office for National Statistics.

ONS (2020b) 'Which jobs can be done from home?', www.ons.gov.uk/employmentandlabourmarket/peopleinwork/employmentandemployeetypes/articles/whichjobscanbedonefromhome/2020-07-21 (accessed 8 July 2021).

ONS (2021a) *Coronavirus and the Social Impacts on Great Britain: Dataset*, Newport: Office for National Statistics.

ONS (2021b) *Opinions and Lifestyle Survey QMI*, Newport: Office for National Statistics.

Rodríguez, J (2020) *Covid-19 and the Welsh Economy: Working from Home*, Cardiff: Wales Fiscal Analysis.

Tippin, N T and Hilton, M L (eds) (2010) *A Database for a Changing Economy: Review of the Occupational Information Network (O*NET)*, Washington, DC: National Academies Press.

4 Remote Working and the Employer

'We were uniquely positioned to respond quickly and allow folks to work from home given our emphasis on decentralisation and supporting a distributed workforce capable of working from anywhere. The past few months have proven we can make that work', spokeswoman for Jack Dorsey, CEO of Twitter, 11 May 2021.

'It is critical that we are all present in our offices. Some of the best decisions and insights come from hallway and cafeteria discussions, meeting new people, and impromptu team meetings. Speed and quality are often sacrificed when we work from home', internal memo sent by Marissa Mayer, CEO of Yahoo!, 22 February 2013.

4.1 Introduction

There is no shortage of commentary on the advantages and disadvantages of working at home for employers as the quotes at the top of this chapter demonstrate. Some see the benefits of allowing employees the option of working at home and have announced that staff can work remotely from wherever they want. Others want all of their employees on-site so that they can rub shoulders with their managers and colleagues. There is, of course, a third group of employers who are contemplating offering employees the option to work at home (or elsewhere) some of the time if they wish, but insisting that they also come into the office on a regular basis – the so-called hybrid working option.

The aim of this chapter is to examine the issues that employers face and the reasons for these differing attitudes. It will also evaluate the gains and losses of allowing employees greater flexibility to decide where they work in a post-pandemic world. To do so, we outline what theories suggest and assess the strength of the empirical evidence to back them up.

The chapter begins by emphasising the importance that space has traditionally played in the management of labour and hence the challenge that

DOI: 10.4324/9781003247050-4

off-site working brings. The construction of offices and factories, the collection of workers in a single workplace, and their placement at desks and benches within sight of management are not accidental developments. Rather these spatial arrangements form a key feature of how labour has been managed for centuries. It is based on two principles. First, that employees are present at work and therefore do their allotted hours on the employer's premises. Secondly, that they are visible to their managers and/or colleagues while they carry out their work. The growth in working at home poses a challenge to this approach. This can be seen, for example, in the explosion of interest in surveillance software during the pandemic and a desire to make workers electronically visible. However, the chapter presents evidence to suggest that the growth of homeworking is strongest among employers who adopt a more trusting approach to managing their staff. The chapter goes on to consider the theoretical reasons why some employers are in favour of homeworking and why some are against it. The final substantive section reviews the empirical evidence on what effect the pandemic-induced growth in homeworking had on employee productivity.

4.2 Management Practices

We need to begin by remembering that industrialisation created two new and distinct spheres of social and economic life – home and work. Previously, these overlapped and were difficult to differentiate. Before the industrial revolution, farms, workshops, manor houses, and palaces were both places of work and places to live. Employers quickly realised that this spatial arrangement was no longer fit for a world of increasing output, greater specialisation, and a capitalist class keen on extracting more output from each worker. This meant that embezzlement needed to be minimised, productivity needed to be raised, and processes needed to be better coordinated. Housing workers in factories and allocating individual workers to specific locations in which they were required to do their tasks was the architectural solution (Baldry, 1999; Baldry *et al.*, 1998; Marglin, 1976; Felstead *et al.*, 2003).

Workplaces therefore came to comprise designated places for particular individuals performing specific functions. This architectural arrangement made possible processes of monitoring, observation, and surveillance, with their associated disciplines and opportunities for regulation (Foucault, 1977). Early factories were designed with surveillance in mind. This ensured that managers could, at a moment's notice, watch what individual workers were doing, but workers were never quite sure when they were being watched. Known as the panopticon, this architectural arrangement meant that workers controlled their own behaviour for fear of being caught acting inappropriately. The potential of observation – or the normalising gaze – was enough to ensure that in the factory context products were not stolen, machines were not tampered with, and that workers did not slack. However, the normalising gaze was never total and employees – individually and collectively – have been able to resist total managerial control.

These historical developments are usually discussed in relation to factory workers. However, as with the assembly line, managerial control was also built into the fabric of the office and the allocation of workers to desks. Like the factory, then, the office also constitutes a personal place of work. This might take the form of a walled cell (cellular office) or, particularly from the 1960s onwards, a desk in an open-plan office. Either way, each worker has their own tiny plot or cube of space dedicated to their use. Staff not 'in the office' are, by definition, not 'at work' and are not eligible for payment. Equally, staff who 'put in the hours' in the designated location are deemed worthy of reward and promotion. Like factory workers, office workers too signal that they are working by being present and visible to their managers and/or colleagues.

The cubes of space occupied by office workers are never, of course, their personal property. Nevertheless, employees often develop a strong sense of personal identification with 'their' office space. As a result, they often personalise their working environment with pictures, plants, photographs, souvenirs, and other memorabilia. Although they have no legal title to their offices, they are able to colonise symbolically the space of their employment.

The visibility and presence of office workers are, therefore, double-edged weapons in the armoury of management. By occupying the sites that they have been allocated, office workers are open to managerial regulation, control, and disciplinary gaze. At the same time, by symbolically personalising their designated cubes of space, office workers differentiate themselves from less privileged members of the workforce and project their own identities into the world of employment.

However, some ways of earning a living do not entail attendance at a workplace. For example, some members of the sales force – 'commercial travellers' or 'road warriors' – go out visiting customers to sell products of various kinds (Spears, 1995). Many self-employed people run small businesses in premises where they live, including small hotels, corner shops, guest houses, and pubs (Honsden, 1984; Hawkins and Radcliffe, 1971). Some of those doing low-paid routine manual and clerical jobs work at home (Felstead and Jewson, 1996, 2000; Boris, 1994; Boris and Daniels, 1989; Boris and Prügl, 1996). However, industrial homeworking is far less widespread today. Even at its height, their numbers were relatively small compared with those who commute to and from an office to conduct their daily tasks at a designated desk.

The potentiality for more and more office work to be carried out away from the office was a strengthening trend evident in the data well before the pandemic (see Chapter 3). This meant that the completion of office work no longer required staff to be present in designated buildings at particular times of the day or week. Instead, such work can be carried out using electronic technologies that make possible communication – in word, image and speech – with co-workers and clients who are geographically remote. Smartphones, email, laptop computers, and video conferencing mean that many aspects of office work can be carried out anywhere and at any time. As long as workers are connected, it is no longer necessary to 'go into the office' in order to carry out many office tasks.

That said, not all aspects of employment relations can be conducted in this way. There remains a crucial role for face-to-face interactions in the form of formal meetings and informal social contacts (Boden and Molotch, 1994). Nevertheless, a large proportion of office tasks can be done through the use of information and communications technology (ICT). These devices also make it possible to work in ways that are profoundly different from those of the past. In particular, the idea that some spaces and times are ring-fenced for work and others for non-work can be swept away. In principle, it is possible to work remotely – at home, in a hotel, motorway service station, or airport lounge, or while in transit on a train, plane, or in a car. Furthermore, it is possible to 'log on' at any time – weekends and evenings, holidays and festivals, family celebrations and dinner parties with friends. The times and places of employment can weave their way into and through all the nooks and crannies of our lives. The relationship between the spaces and times of work and non-work are no longer sequential, linear, and chronological but, instead, are becoming a dispersed mosaic of ubiquitous connections that are available around the clock. The pandemic-induced rise in homeworking has meant that many more people have experienced these changes first-hand.

Management has responded in one of two ways to the challenges of managing a dispersed workforce. It has either sought to recreate the visibility and presence of workers in a number of ways or trusted those working at home to 'deliver the goods' while out of sight. Both approaches are considered in what follows.

Previous research suggests that some employers have sought to make the activities of their homeworking staff visible through the collection of documentary performance data and/or the use of technological devices (Felstead, Jewson *et al.*, 2005). One tactic is to require homeworkers to complete time sheets in order to document their hours. However, these texts are open to distortion and misrepresentation. For example, workers can easily manipulate time sheets in order to disguise their pattern of working and to give the impression that their activities are spread out evenly throughout the week.

Another approach is to introduce new surveillance devices and/or activate the surveillance capabilities of those already in use. In this context, the surveillance potentiality of the factory or office layout is replaced by the 'electronic panopticon' (Sewell and Wilkinson, 1992; Bain and Taylor, 2000). Previous research, for example, has revealed circumstances in which computers are used to count individual keystrokes, to monitor time spent on and away from the keyboard, to check on the kind of work being done, and to assess how quickly staff are carrying out their tasks (e.g. Huws, 1984; Ford, 1999; Lankshear *et al.*, 2001). In these cases, homeworkers know they can be watched, but they do not know when they are being watched and how frequently. As a result, they act as though they are under constant surveillance.

In these cases, workers' outputs rather than workers themselves are being watched. Yet, we know from other research that sight is the most powerful and revealing of all the senses. This hierarchy is reflected in everyday speech. For example, we claim to 'see' something that is said once it is understood; those who do not or refuse to do so are said to have 'blind spots'; long-term thinkers are regarded as 'visionaries'; and academics aim to 'illuminate' or 'shed new light' on their chosen subject (Urry, 2000a, 2000b: chapter 4). In the light of this, some employers have gone a step further by taking screenshots of their workers' computers and/or activating the computer's in-built camera to watch what their staff are doing when they are working at home.

While this might seem far-fetched, companies supplying such technology report a spike in demand for their services. The US-based company, Hubstaff, reported that its sales rose fourfold during the pandemic. Another company, Sneek, offers technology that takes photographs of workers through their laptops and uploads them for colleagues to see, with shoots taken as often as every minute. Its sales rose fivefold with the firm reporting to have 20,000 clients in the UK (BBC News, 2020). According to a YouGov survey of around 2,000 employers carried out in November 2020, 12% were using software to monitor staff working at home in a variety of ways and a further 8% were planning to do so (Skillcast, 2020). However, the legality of these forms of surveillance, without informing employees, is questionable and their use suggests that employers feel that some of their staff cannot be trusted. Nevertheless, according to a survey carried out between October 2020 and March 2021, a large minority (44.9%) of over 3,000 employees report that their work activities were monitored by management via the automated systems built into everyday devices (Taylor *et al.*, 2021).

An alternative management approach is to trust workers to deliver the goods. Managers, using this approach, monitor outputs rather than inputs to the labour process (Department of Trade and Industry, 2000; Dwelly, 2000). This, therefore, entails managers setting a series of short- to medium-term targets, the completion of which represents a rolling picture of employee performance.

The Management and Expectations Survey (MES) suggests that such firms were better able to switch to homeworking during the pandemic. This survey was conducted in 2016 and 2020 (Awano *et al.*, 2018; Schneebacher *et al.*, 2021a). On both occasions, plant managers working in businesses employing ten or more were asked 12 closed questions about target setting, monitoring, and the disciplining of staff. This approach takes its inspiration from the Management and Organisational Practices Survey (MOPS) carried out initially by the US Census Bureau. It has been replicated in countries across the world (Sadun *et al.*, 2017). In 2020, respondents were asked to report on the situation when they were surveyed and in the year before the pandemic began. In addition, they were asked what proportion of managers and non-managers worked remotely.

This survey, then, focuses on the quality of management practices as a whole and not on how those working at home in particular were managed. The survey gathers data on how well management: reacts to problems; uses key performance indicators and targets; enhances employee performance; and deals with staff who are not performing well enough. Those employers which have a high management score, and are therefore deemed better managed, report that more of their staff were working at home in 2020 than in 2019. Moreover, this holds after controlling for other factors such as industry, region, establishment size, and qualification level. It is also substantive: a one percentage change in the management score is associated with a ten percentage point increase in the prevalence of homeworking (Schneebacher *et al.*, 2021b).

4.3 Theoretical Perspectives

Unlike any other factor of production, such as machines and raw materials, the amount of work workers do cannot be fixed in advance. Workers sell their capacity to work to employers, not what they produce and so labour is more than just a commodity. It, therefore, follows that the precise nature of the labour input, or more specifically the tasks the worker is expected to perform, can never be perfectly specified ahead of time. In economics, this is referred to as the principal–agent problem. It occurs when one party takes action (the agent) on behalf of the other (principal). In the work context, the employee is contracted to carry out work for the employer, but the effort they put in is not predetermined and cannot always be measured. It is for this reason that disciplinary procedures, financial rewards and penalties, and/or the threat of dismissal are put in place to deter workers from shirking or failing to meet the required standards. As outlined earlier, the buildings where people work can also be used to control behaviour and monitor performance. It is on these grounds that employers have traditionally been fearful of remote working which puts employees out of direct sight.

Another fear is that off-site employees will not be able to learn from others. Therefore, their productivity as well as the productivity of colleagues who are no longer around them will fall. This is based on a conceptualisation that views learning as much wider than the number of times someone goes on a training course, for how long and at what cost. Most notably, this is encapsulated in the term 'learning as participation' as distinct from 'learning as acquisition' (Sfard, 1998). The former refers to a conceptualisation that views learning as a process in which employees improve their productivity by watching, listening, and following how colleagues deal with everyday tasks (Sfard, 1998). These informal, unplanned, and incidental exchanges of tacit knowledge are situated in everyday encounters which cannot easily be reproduced remotely. The latter perspective, on the other hand, views learning as a product with a visible, identifiable outcome, often accompanied by certification or proof of attendance (Felstead, Fuller *et al.*, 2005).

Increased geographical dispersion of workers from one another can have further drawbacks. For example, it makes the induction of newcomers into a community of practitioners more difficult (Jewson, 2008). Physical proximity with co-workers facilitates serendipitous contacts and promotes non-verbal communication through body language, eye contact, and touching rituals, such as the handshake or during the pandemic elbow bumps and fist pumps. However, this problem can be overcome, at least in part, by the scheduling of face-to-face interactions between colleagues, clients, and superiors. Some organisations with working at home schemes before the pandemic took this a stage further by requiring employees to spend time on-site prior to being formally based off-site (Felstead *et al.*, 2003). Post-pandemic organisations may require all workers to be on-site for at least some of the time, hence the interest in hybrid working (see Chapter 6).

However, difficulties remain. First, the impact and relevance of attitudes and information transmitted in the early stages of employment gradually diminish over time and may need to be updated. Initial on-site induction offers a fixed reference point that can become dated. Even regular, but not daily, on-site attendance means that the learning opportunities that co-presence brings are reduced. Secondly, for on-site induction to be effective, a substantial proportion of the workforce – old-timers need to induct newcomers – also have to be physically present. Similarly, hybrid working requires that all team members need to be physically present on the same day of the week for intra-team learning and bonding to occur. Thirdly, a requirement that all staff report on-site may not be helpful in wooing potential recruits from further afield who may be attracted by remote working without any need to be physically present at a particular site.

Similarly, remote working can hamper the development of trust between managers and their staff. Trust occurs when individuals strive to meet any commitments they give in good faith, provide an honest account of the circumstances in which those commitments are given, and do not take advantage of others when the opportunity arises (Cummings and Bromley, 1996). Several factors, such as shared social norms, repeated interactions, and shared experiences facilitate the development of trust. Physical co-location can reinforce social similarity, shared values, and expectations. Face-to-face encounters are considered crucial for building trust and increasing individual and collective levels of performance.

On this basis, it is claimed that information technology alone is not a sufficient basis on which to develop high levels of trust (Handy, 1995; Jarvenpaa and Leidner, 1999). Instead, some degree of physical co-location is needed for trust to be built up and then reinforced through virtual communications such as video calls:

> To start establishing a relationship I think you do need to have the physical contact more because you have this indefinable thing about relationships and body language and you don't get it in the same way, so my view is as you do the team building you need to have some physical contact and then you use video conferencing to reinforce that in between all these physical sessions.
>
> (manager quoted in Nandhakumar and Baskerville, 2006: 381)

Some theories, on the other hand, predict that homeworking can boost performance. Social exchange theory, for example, has been used by organisational theorists to explain the motivations behind employee behaviours and attitudes (Gouldner, 1960; Blau, 1964). The theory is based on the idea that parties must abide by certain rules and norms of exchange that generate reciprocity (Cropanzano and Mitchell, 2005). In this context, the theory suggests that in exchange for being allowed to work at home (and having their jobs protected especially during the pandemic) employees do more not less. This includes doing unpaid work, working harder in order to get noticed or putting in extra effort out of obligation to the employer and/or office-bound colleagues (Elsbach *et al.*, 2012; Golden, 2007; Kelliher and Anderson, 2011). All this is designed to show that they are not taking the opportunity to take advantage. For example, by watching daytime television, sunbathing, painting the house, going to the gym, or engaging in other non-work pursuits.

The different nature of job tasks, too, can have a major bearing on where they are best carried out. Previous research shows that mobile workers, for example, have to mould their work activities around what is possible and acceptable in different venues (Dant and Martin, 2001; Laurier, 2001; Felstead *et al.*, 2005: chapter 6). This can be seen in some adverts prompting the virtues of air travel and the downsides of communication by phone. The British Airways 'ever shaken phones on a deal' poster campaign is a classic example of this approach. It showed two pin-striped suited arms about to shake on a deal but with phones replacing hands. It gets the message across that there is more to person-to-person interaction than voice alone. This is more than just an advertising gimmick; it is based on evidence that people prefer to communicate face-to-face. If this is not possible, a second best solution is found: a video call, for example, is considered to be better than a telephone call and a swift email better than a letter. However, these are weak substitutes for co-presence which is 'thick' with meaning communicated through facial gestures, body language, voice intonation, eye contact, and so on (Boden and Molotch, 1994; Urry, 2002; Reades and Crookston, 2021).

There are also some activities – such as writing a book, preparing a presentation, analysing data, or reading long documents – that are best carried out without interruption and disturbance from office chatter and noise. In fact, spending time doing these activities at home is likely to be more productive and not less. However, tasks that are more tedious and dull are better carried out in the office, where office chatter and noise can be used to tame the boredom involved (Banbury and Berry, 1998; Dutcher, 2012).

4.4 Empirical Evidence

Despite theories to the contrary, employers have long feared that off-site working – whether at home or elsewhere – would result in productivity levels falling. This is hardly surprising given the importance traditionally placed by employers on making employees visible at all times to management. It is important, therefore, to consider the empirical evidence on the effect that homeworking has on productivity, both before and during the pandemic.

We start with one of the most rigorous studies. It focused on the airfare and hotel booking departments of a leading Chinese travel agency, Ctrip, based in Shanghai. The study was carried out over several years stretching from November 2010 to May 2013. The researchers, which included the CEO of Ctrip, were 'granted exceptional access not only to data but also to Ctrip management's thinking about the experiment and its results' (Bloom *et al.*, 2015: 171). The nine-month experiment was a randomised control trial of call centre workers.

Traditionally, these workers sat together in teams according to their roles, often occupying an entire aisle. There were teams who took orders from clients, those who liaised with airlines and hotels, and those who solved problems. When logged on, calls were automatically routed to available operators according to their function. Each call centre operator worked in their own cubicle with equipment including a computer, a telephone, and a headset. Team leaders patrolled the aisles to monitor employees' performance, and provide help and support when necessary.

For the experiment, workers were put into two groups: those working at home (the treatment group) and those remaining in the office (the control group). The treatment group was required to work four days a week at home and one day a week in the office – in fact, operating as hybrid workers (see Chapter 2). To ensure comparability, they worked the same schedule and under the same team leader as their office-bound counterparts. Both groups also used the same computer terminals, communications equipment, and software. However, those working at home were not allowed to substitute reduced commuting time – estimated to be 80 minutes daily – for increased overtime. Nevertheless, entire teams could change their hours to cope with, for example, increased demand for their services.

Participation in the experiment was voluntary. Around half of the 994 call operators agreed to take part in the trial. Of these, 249 were deemed qualified to work at home by virtue of having at least six months' tenure, broadband access, and a private room at home in which they could work. Those qualified to take part were, then, divided randomly into the treatment and control groups discussed earlier.

The experiment produced striking results. The working at home group outperformed office-bound workers by 13%. This came about by increasing the hours spent logged onto the system during shifts and increasing the number of calls taken per minute. Both are examples of intensive work effort; that is, reducing the 'porosity' of the working day by reducing the gaps between tasks during which the body or mind rests. This was explained by two main factors: the greater convenience of being at home (e.g. the ease of making a tea or coffee, or using the toilet); and the relative quietness of the home environment.

Moreover, at the end of the experiment, all of those working in the call centre were allowed to choose whether they wanted to continue working at home, switch back, or start working at home for the first time. There was significant movement in all of these directions. Around half of the treatment group returned to the office after the experiment, despite lengthy and costly commutes. About a third of the control group elected to work at home, and around one in ten workers who did not volunteer to take part in the experiment elected to work at home. These selection effects further boosted productivity with the least productive choosing to return to the office as homeworking was not for them. On the other hand, the most productive decided to remain working at home or become homeworkers for the first time. The end result was that homeworking boosted productivity.

Despite the rigour of the Bloom *et al.* (2015) study, its results cannot be read off as directly comparable to a situation of people being enforced to work at home in order to limit the spread of coronavirus or a post-pandemic future of more off-site working. First, the study was based on a specific group of relatively low-paid workers whose productivity can be measured in great detail. Jobs which are more creative and rely on the input of others may be more difficult to carry out productively at home. This includes many of those who carried out work at home during the pandemic (cf. Chapter 3). Secondly, the experiment was voluntary, so that those choosing to take part were, by definition, more disposed to this way of working. They were not being asked to work at home whether they liked it or not.

Thirdly, volunteers had to meet certain eligibility criteria. These were employment with the company for a minimum of six months, a good internet connection, and a separate room in which to work. These conditions applied after the experiment had ended and working at home was rolled out across the company. This is different again to the circumstances during the pandemic when homeworking was adopted as an emergency measure. Workers had to convert their bedrooms into offices, their living room tables into desks, and their kitchens into places of work. Working at home also meant that they were competing for space within the home. At this time, other household members were also working at home, undergraduate students were learning remotely, and school-aged children, too, were studying at home either because schools were shut or they were self-isolating. However, as Bloom (2014: 4) himself remarked before the pandemic: 'Any disruption that offers a chance to have people work remotely is an opportunity to see how effective they are off-site'. The instruction to work at home if you can, then, represents a much wider experiment of the effect of homeworking on productivity. It is to this evidence that we now turn.

One of the earliest UK studies to investigate the impact that the spike in homeworking was having on productivity was the Understanding Society Covid-19 Study. This survey consists of nine surveys carried out between April 2020 and September 2021. A total of 6,000–7,000 workers in the UK took part in each survey. They are asked how often they worked at home in the four weeks before completing the online survey (Institute for Social and Economic Research, 2021; Felstead and Reuschke, 2021; Etheridge *et al.*, 2020).

Respondents were asked to report where they were working in January/ February 2020. They were also asked where they were working in the four weeks before being interviewed. Those who reported that they recently worked at home sometimes, often, or always to the June 2020 version of the survey were then asked: 'Please think about how much work you get done per hour these days. How does that compare to how much you would have got done *per hour* back in January/February 2020 [and if they did not work at home in January/February 2020, a memory jogger was added] when, according to what you have previously told us, you were not working from home?' (original emphasis). The data collected allow a 'then and now' productivity comparison to be made. The same question was also asked of all respondents in three further versions of the survey.

The results suggest that two-fifths (40.9%) of employees in June 2020 reported that they were able to get as much work done then as they did six months earlier. Over a quarter (28.9%) said that they got more done, while 30.2% said that their productivity had fallen. On the whole, then, home-working in the early part of the pandemic did not appear to have had a significant effect on productivity levels. Other employee-level studies reveal a similar pattern. For example, a survey of almost 5,000 UK residents carried out in January and February 2021 found over three-quarters reported that they were at least as productive when they worked at home than when they did not (Taneja *et al.*, 2021).

Furthermore, the Understanding Society Covid-19 Study results suggest that productivity did not drop as restrictions continued. In fact, proportionately more homeworkers reported that their productivity had either remained the same or risen since the pandemic began in both the September 2020 and January 2021 surveys. Continued high levels of homeworking during the pandemic did not appear to be a drag on productivity. In fact, a sizeable minority reported that the change of work location had little effect on how much they could accomplish per hour (see Figure 4.1).

Like the Bloom *et al.* (2015) study, the results of this pandemic study also suggest that the selection effects may serve to boost productivity when employees can volunteer to work at home rather than everyone being told to do so. Those with the lowest self-reported levels of productivity in the study reported the strongest desire to return to the office. On the other hand, those with the highest productivity levels were keen to continue to work at home even when social restrictions are fully lifted (Felstead and Reuschke, 2021:

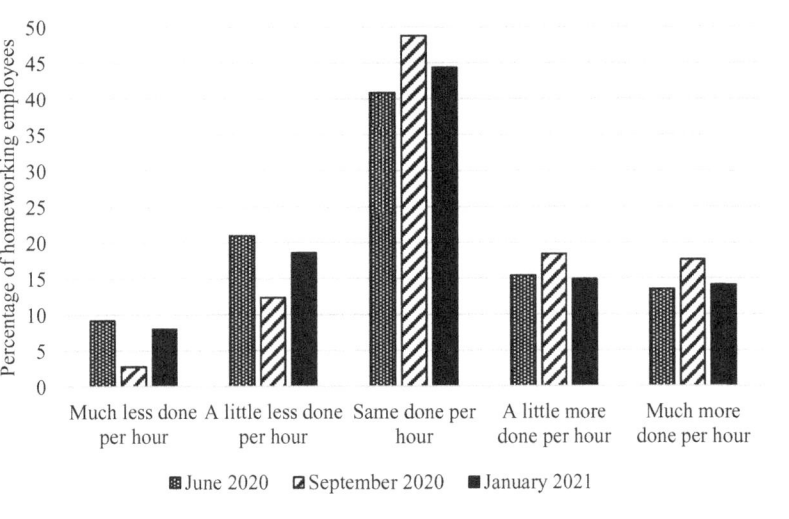

Figure 4.1 Self-reported Productivity Effects of Employees Working at Home During the Pandemic in the UK

Source: Own calculations from the Understanding Society Covid-19 Study, June 2020, September 2020, and January 2021

Table 5). This sorting effect means that increased levels of homeworking in the future may boost rather than reduce productivity levels.

Those who reported that their productivity had changed since January/ February 2020 were asked to identify the main reason for the change. Nearly half of full-time homeworkers (45.8%) put the increase in their productivity down to fewer interruptions and around three out of ten (27.8%) put it down to not having to commute to and from work. Those who did none of their work at home but who reported an increase in their productivity gave different reasons. Having to do more work came top of the list (49.4%).

Different reasons were given for falls in productivity. Of those doing all of their work at home, the three main reasons given were lack of motivation (31.6%), more interruptions (21.5%), and equipment difficulties (11.4%). These factors were barely mentioned by those who did not work at home. For these employees, the three main reasons for the fall were 'other factors' (35.9%) followed by less work to do (21.6%) and the requirement to be at work (11.1%).

Furthermore, the main reason for falling productivity varied by gender with female homeworkers more likely than men to cite interruptions from family members. While this is outside the control of management, the finding that the lack of motivation and poor equipment can hinder home-workers' productivity is something that management can address with better communication, regular meetings, and more investment in information technology. These findings are echoed by others using a broader range of research methods such as qualitative interviews with homeworkers themselves and their employers (e.g. Skountridaki *et al.*, 2020; Bevan, 2020; Parry, 2020; Morris and Hassard, 2020).

However, a significant drawback of this study is that it relies on respondents reporting on their own productivity levels and making comparisons with the past. These perceptions may be upwardly biased. Employees may overstate their productivity to prove – to themselves and others – that they can cope with working at home and/or to increase the chances that they will have the option to work in this way in the future. Another possibility is that despite being asked to focus on what they can get done per hour, they actually report on their output levels and not on their output per hour.

A study of over 10,000 professionals working in a large Asian information technology service company provides support for this suggestion (Gibbs *et al.*, 2021). The study is based on data gathered over a 17-month period from April 2019 through to August 2020. It, therefore, covers the period before and after employees were told to work at home (i.e. 15 March 2020), but not the period when employees started to return to work in the office (October 2020). Employees' output was tracked throughout this period. The precise nature of the output measure varied according to job role. However, the company uses a normalised measure of output to make different jobs and roles comparable. For example, the output of programmers is measured by the number of programming tasks completed divided by the number of tasks assigned. For other roles, output is measured by the number of reviews of code completed relative to the monthly target, or the number of reports delivered relative to a set target. The study also analysed the activities employees did during their working hours. These activities included meeting with clients, collaborating with other colleagues, developing new software or hardware applications, and networking with colleagues inside and outside the firm. The study followed the same employees over this period, the output produced, the hours worked, and the activities undertaken. The results reveal that output barely changed, but employees who worked longer hours spent more time using the keyboard or mouse and considerably more time in online meetings. As a result, productivity actually declined, particularly among those with children who worked long hours to compensate and keep their output levels up.

Nevertheless, evidence gathered from employers in general suggest that productivity was not reduced by the increase in homeworking. For example, in September 2020 an ONS survey asked 5,500 employers about the effect that homeworking was having on employees' productivity (ONS, 2020). A majority said that productivity had not changed (51.9%), but around a quarter (23.9%) said that productivity had fallen and a similar proportion said it had either increased or that they did not know what effect it had had (24.3%). Furthermore, there is evidence of a correlation between the intention to make homeworking a permanent feature of the employment offer and the experience of homeworking on productivity (Haskel, 2021: Figure 5). The more positive the impact the more likely firms are to offer it in the future.

Other employer surveys suggest that productivity was not reduced by the pandemic-induced surge in working at home. For example, the Chartered Institute of Personnel and Development (CIPD) conducted a survey of 1,046 establishments. It found that around a third of employers (37%) said that homeworking had made no difference to employee productivity. A similar proportion of employers reported that it had either a small positive effect (18%) or a small negative effect (22%). A smaller share of employers perceived stronger impacts, again in both directions, with 11% reporting strong positive effects and 6% strong negative effects (Brinkley *et al.*, 2020: 14–17).

Employers have another motivation for greater use of homeworking – savings made from not having to house large numbers of workers in office buildings that they either rent or buy and have to heat and maintain. Indeed, one of the initial motivations for the call centre experiment in Bloom *et al.* (2015) was the reduction in the costs of office rent, which were increasing rapidly due to the booming real estate market in Shanghai. In fact, two-thirds of the savings made from the experimental shift towards homeworking came from a reduction in office costs.

UK employers, too, are looking to make similar savings. The Institute of Directors (IoD) carried out a survey in September 2020 of around 1,000 company directors. More than half said they were planning to reduce their long-term use of office space and more than one in five reported their usage would be significantly lower (IoD, 2020). Similarly, a survey of 573 businesses carried out by the CBI suggests that employers are planning for higher levels of homeworking than in the past. As a result, they expected to reduce their office space by 18% by 2024 (CBI, 2020: 4–5).

4.5 Conclusion

Employers have traditionally gathered employees in one place – the factory or the office. This required employees to present for a fixed number of hours each week and to be visible to their superiors and/or colleagues for much of this time. However, offices are costly to build and maintain.

Even before the pandemic, off-site working was a growing phenomenon (cf. Chapter 3). More workers were trusted to pull their weight or monitored by their output and not according to their physical presence in the building. The coronavirus pandemic accelerated the shift towards off-site working and the greater use of the home in particular.

By and large, existing evidence suggests that the shift did not reduce productivity levels, at least in the UK. However, the international evidence is not as clear-cut. An online survey of workers in the Netherlands, for example, found that respondents were 'slightly less productive' working at home during the pandemic than they were before restrictions were introduced (Rubin *et al.*, 2020: 2). Another online survey this time of Japanese workers revealed that while self-reported productivity levels were lower when working at home, this varied by prior experience of homeworking and the nature of the job. Highly educated and well-paid workers, who used to commute long journeys to work before the pandemic, reported a smaller drop-off in their productivity (Morikawa, 2020).

On the other hand, a Canadian study of workers suggests the reverse with a third of respondents reporting that their productivity had increased, not fallen, since they were told to work at home (Saba *et al.*, 2020). Another Canadian study – based on data taken from a supplement to the Canadian Labour Force Survey – found that nine out of ten workers who had not worked at home before the pandemic reported being just as productive as they were previously. However, it also revealed variation. For example, couples with children less frequently reported being able to do more per hour than couples without children (Mehdi and Morisette, 2021). Similarly, a US survey of 653 business owners carried out in March/April 2020 suggests that productivity effects vary by industry and the educational level of those involved (Bartik *et al.*, 2020).

Regardless of what happens to productivity, homeworking may be detrimental to job quality. The next chapter, therefore, focuses on the impact that homeworking – and remote working more generally – can have on various aspects of non-pecuniary job quality. These include the impact that changes to the location of work can have on work–life balance, the intensity of work, promotion and development opportunities, health and safety, and, ultimately, employee well-being.

References

Awano, G, Bloom, N, Dolby, T, Mizen, P, Riley, R, Senga, T, Vyas, J and Wales, P (2018) *Management Practices and Productivity in British Production and Services Industries – Initial Results from the Management and Expectations Survey: 2016*, Newport: Office for National Statistics.

Bain, P and Taylor, P (2000) 'Entrapped by the "electronic panopticon"? Worker resistance in the call centre', *New Technology, Work and Employment*, 15(1): 2–18.

Baldry, C (1999) 'Space – the final frontier', *Sociology*, 33(3): 535–553.

Baldry, C, Bain, P and Taylor, P (1998) 'Bright Satanic offices: intensification, control and team Taylorism', in Thompson, P and Warhurst, C (eds) *Workplaces of the Future*, London: Palgrave Macmillan.

Banbury, S and Berry, D C (1998) 'Disruption of office-related tasks by speech and office noise', *British Journal of Psychology*, 89(3): 499–517.

Bartik, A W, Cullen, Z B, Glaeser, E L, Luca, M and Stanton, C T (2020) *What Jobs Can Be Done at Home During the Covid-19 Crisis? Evidence from Firm-Level Surveys*, NBER Working Paper Series, Working Paper, No. 27422, Cambridge, MA: National Bureau of Economic Research.

BBC News (2020) 'I monitor my staff with software that takes screenshots, by Lora Jones', 22 September, www.bbc.co.uk/news/business-54289152 (accessed 14 July 2021).

Bevan, S (2020) 'Interim survey results: local government survey', presented at the Work at Home: Transitions and Tensions Seminar, 10 December, https://business.senedd.wales/documents/s500006852/Remote%20working%20report%20Professor%20Alan%20Felstead.pdf.

Blau, P (1964) *Power and Exchange in Social Life*, New York: John Wiley & Sons.

Bloom, N (2014) 'To raise productivity, let more employees work from home', *Harvard Business Review Magazine*: 1–7, January–February.

Bloom, N, Liang, J, Roberts, J and Ying, Z J (2015) 'Does working from home work? Evidence from a Chinese experiment', *Quarterly Journal of Economics*, 130(1): 165–218.

Boden, D and Molotch, H (1994) 'The compulsion to proximity', in Friedland, R and Boden, D (eds) *Nowhere: Space, Time and Modernity*, Berkeley: University of California Press.

Boris, E (1994) *Home to Work: Motherhood and the Politics of Industrial Homework in the United States*, Cambridge: Cambridge University Press.

Boris, E and Daniels, C R (eds) (1989) *Homework: Historical and Contemporary Perspectives on Paid Labour at Home*, Urbana: University of Illinois Press.

Boris, E and Prügl, E (1996) *Homeworkers in Global Perspective: Invisible No More*, London: Routledge.

Brinkley, I, Willmott, B, Beatson, M and Davies, G (2020) *Embedding New Ways of Working*, London: Chartered Institute of Personnel and Development.

CBI (2020) *No Turning Back*, London: Confederation of British Industry.

Cropanzano, R and Mitchell, M S (2005) 'Social exchange theory: an interdisciplinary review', *Journal of Management*, 31(6): 874–900.

Cummings, L L and Bromley, P (1996) 'The organizational trust inventory (OTI): development and validation', in Kramer, R M and Tyler, T R (eds) *Trust in Organizations: Frontiers of Theory and Research*, Thousand Oaks, CA: Sage.

Dant, T and Martin, P J (2001) 'By car: carrying modern society', in Gronow, J and Warde, A (eds) *Ordinary Consumption*, London: Routledge.

Department of Trade and Industry (2000) *Working Anywhere: Exploring Telework for Individuals and Organisations* (2nd Edition), London: DTI.

Dutcher, E G (2012) 'The effects of telecommuting on productivity: an experimental examination, the role of dull and creative tasks', *Journal of Economic Behavior and Organization*, 84(1): 355–363.

Dwelly, T (2000) *Living at Work: A New Policy Framework for Modern Homeworkers*, York: Joseph Rowntree Foundation.

Elsbach, K D, Cable, D M and Sherman, J W (2012) 'How passive "face time" affects perceptions of employees: evidence of spontaneous trait inference', *Human Relations*, 63(6): 735–760.

Etheridge, B, Wang, Y and Tang, L (2020) *Worker-Productivity During Lockdown and Working from Home: Evidence from Self-Reports*, ISER Working Paper Series, No. 2020-12, Colchester: Institute for Social and Economic Research, University of Essex.

Felstead, A, Fuller, A, Unwin, L, Ashton, D, Butler, P and Lee, T (2005) 'Surveying the scene: learning metaphors, survey design and the workplace context', *Journal of Education and Work*, 18(4): 359–383.

Felstead, A and Jewson, N (1996) *Homeworkers in Britain*, London: HMSO.

Felstead, A and Jewson, N (2000) *In Work, at Home: Towards an Understanding of Homeworking*, London: Routledge.

Felstead, A, Jewson, N and Walters, S (2003) 'Managerial control of employees working at home', *British Journal of Industrial Relations*, 41(2): 241–264.

Felstead, A, Jewson, N and Walters, S (2005) *Changing Places of Work*, Basingstoke: Palgrave Macmillan.

Felstead, A and Reuschke, D (2021) 'A flash in the pan or a permanent change? The growth of homeworking during the pandemic and its effect on employee productivity in the UK', *Information Technology and People*, online early view.

Ford, M (1999) *Surveillance and Privacy at Work*, London: Institute of Employment Rights.

Foucault, M (1977) *Discipline and Punish*, Harmondsworth: Penguin, Peregrine Books.

Gibbs, M, Mengel, F and Siemroth, C (2021) *Work from Home and Productivity: Evidence from Personnel and Analytics Data on IT Professionals*, Becker Friedman Institute Working Paper, No. 56, Chicago: Becker Friedman Institute.

Golden, T (2007) 'Co-workers who telework and the impact on those in the office: understanding the implications of virtual work for co-worker satisfaction and turnover intentions', *Human Relations*, 60(11): 1641–1667.

Gouldner, A (1960) 'The norm of reciprocity', *American Sociological Review*, 25(2): 161–178.

Handy, C (1995) 'Trust and the virtual organization', *Harvard Business Review*, 73(3): 40–50.

Haskel, J (2021) 'What is the future of working from home?', *Economics Observatory*, 20 April, www.economicsobservatory.com/what-is-the-future-of-working-from-home (accessed 19 July 2021).

Hawkins, K and Radcliffe, R (1971) 'Competition in the brewing industry', *Journal of Industrial Economics*, 20(1): 20–41.

Honsden, J (1984) *Franchising and Other Business Relationships in Hotel and Catering Services*, London: Heinemann.

Huws, U (1984) *The New Homeworkers: New Technology and the Changing Location of White-Collar Work*, London: Low Pay Unit.

Institute for Social and Economic Research (2021) *Understanding Society COVID-19 User Guide: Version 6.0*, Colchester: University of Essex, January.

IoD (2020) 'Home-working here to stay, new IoD figures suggest', *Press Release*, 5 October, www.iod.com/news/news/articles/Home-working-here-to-stay-new-IoD-figures-suggest (accessed 19 July 2021).

Jarvenpaa, S L and Leidner, D E (1999) 'Communication and trust in global virtual teams', *Organization Science*, 10(6): 791–815.

Jewson, N (2008) 'Communities of practice in their place: some implications of changes in the spatial location of work', in Hughes, J, Jewson, N and Unwin, L (eds) *Communities of Practice: Critical Perspectives*, London: Routledge.

Kelliher, C and Anderson, D (2011) 'Doing more with less? Flexible working practices and the intensification of work', *Human Relations*, 63(1): 83–106.

Lankshear, G, Cook, P, Mason, D, Coates, S and Button, G (2001) 'Call centre employee's responses to electronic monitoring: some research findings', *Work, Employment and Society*, 15(3): 595–605.

Laurier, E (2001) 'Why people say where they are during mobile phone calls', *Environment and Planning D: Society and Space*, 19: 485–504.

Marglin, S (1976) 'What do bosses do?', in Gorz, A (ed) *The Division of Labour*, Brighton: Harvester.

Mehdi, T and Morisette, R (2021) *Working from Home: Productivity and Preferences*, Ottawa: Statistics Canada.

Morikawa, M (2020) *Productivity of Working from Home During the COVID-19 Pandemic: Evidence from an Employee Survey*, RIETI Discussion Paper Series, No. 20-E-073, Tokyo: Research Institute of Economy, Trade and Industry.

Morris, J and Hassard, J (2020) *Home Working? The Present and Future of How and Where We Work in the Context of COVID-19*, Cardiff Business School Working Paper, Cardiff: Cardiff University Business School.

Nandhakumar, J and Baskerville, R (2006) 'Durability of online teamworking: patterns of trust', *Information Technology and People*, 19(4): 371–389.

ONS (2020) *Coronavirus and the Economic Impacts on the UK*, Newport: Office for National Statistics, 8 October.

Parry, J (2020) 'Flexible working: lessons from the great work-from-home mass experiment', *The Conversation*, 21 December.

Reades, J and Crookston, M (2021) *What Face-to-Fact Still Matters: The Persistent Power of Cities in the Post-pandemic Era*, Bristol: Bristol University Press.

Rubin, O, Nikolaeva, A, Nello-Deakin, S and te Brömmelstroet, M (2020) *What Can We Learn from the Covid-19 Pandemic About How People Experience Working from Home and Commuting?*, Centre for Urban Studies, University of Amsterdam Working Paper, Amsterdam: Centre for Urban Studies, University of Amsterdam.

Saba, T, Cachat-Rosset, G, Marsan, J, Klarsfeld, A and Carillo, K (2020) *COVID-19 Crisis Triggers Teleworking: A Global Cure or a Short-Term Solution*, Montréal: Université de Montréal.

Sadun, R, Bloom, N and van Reenan, J (2017) 'Why do we undervalue competent management?', *Harvard Business Review*: 120–127, September–October.

Schneebacher, J, Ardanaz-Badia, A, Hilton, Z, Islam, Z and Shafat, M (2021a) *Management Practices in Great Britain: 2016 to 2020*, Newport: Office for National Statistics.

Schneebacher, J, Jones, K and Shafat, M (2021b) *Management Practices, Homeworking and Productivity During the Coronavirus (COVID-19) Pandemic*, Newport: Office for National Statistics.

Sewell, G and Wilkinson, B (1992) '"Someone to watch over me": surveillance, discipline and the just-in-time labour process', *Sociology*, 26(2): 271–289.

Sfard, A (1998) 'On two metaphors for learning and the dangers of choosing just one', *Educational Researcher*, 27(2): 4–13.

Skillcast (2020) 'Remote-working compliance YouGov survey, by Vivek Dodd', 25 November, www.skillcast.com/blog/remote-working-compliance-survey-key-findings (accessed 14 January 2021).

Skountridaki, L, Zschomler, D, Marks, A and Mallett, O (2020) 'Work-life balance for home-based workers amidst a global pandemic', *The Work-Life Bulletin*, 4(2): 16–22.

Spears, T B (1995) *100 Years on the Road: The Travelling Salesman in American Culture*, New Haven: Yale university Press.

Taneja, S, Mizen, P and Bloom, N (2021) 'Working from home is revolutionizing the UK labour market', https://voxeu.org/article/working-home-revolutionising-uk-labour-market (accessed 19 July 2021).

Taylor, P, Scholarios, D and Howcroft, D (2021) *Covid-19 and Working from Home Survey: Preliminary Findings*, Glasgow: University of Strathclyde.

Urry, J (2000a) 'Mobile sociology', *British Journal of Sociology*, 51(1): 185–203.

Urry, J (2000b) *Sociology Beyond Societies: Mobilities for the Twenty-First Century*, London: Routledge.

Urry, J (2002) 'Mobility and proximity', *Sociology*, 36(2): 255–274.

5 Remote Working and the Employee

'Working from home for over a year, at a desk only a few metres away from the TV and the kitchen, with very little natural self-control hasn't been good for my waistline or my time management. Sometimes it's half past midnight and I'm still on the computer', Alexander Holland, computer chip designer, Oxford, 10 May 2021.

'There's a pressure to check emails, jump on video calls and to be on hand at all hours of the day, and it's become harder to draw a line between work and home life', Claire Mullaly, information technology analyst, Northern Ireland, 3 June 2021.

5.1 Introduction

Before the pandemic, job quality was making headlines with policymakers at all levels – internationally, nationally, and regionally – keen to promote good jobs by using whatever means at their disposal. For the last quarter of a century or more, both the International Labour Organisation's (ILO's) and the European Union's (EU's) employment strategies have been based on the idea that having a job does not mean that workers' needs are automatically met since terms and conditions of jobs vary (ILO, 1999; European Commission, 2001). Job quality has also moved up the national agenda in the UK with the former Prime Minister, Theresa May, commissioning the *Taylor Review of Modern Working Practices* (Taylor, 2017). There has also been a spate of local initiatives designed to promote good work in particular localities. These have often been driven by labour-controlled authorities in large urban conurbations such as London, Manchester, and Liverpool (Hurrell *et al.*, 2017). The devolved administrations have also developed pledges and codes designed to drive good employment practice (Welsh Government, 2017; Scottish Government, 2019). Trade unions, too, have launched charters as a campaigning device to highlight employment relations issues in particular sectors such as social care (Moore, 2017).

DOI: 10.4324/9781003247050-5

To some extent this interest has been weakened by the pandemic, but in other respects it has been strengthened. On the one hand, government policies – such as the furlough scheme and 'eat out to help out' initiative – have put the focus on protecting all jobs, regardless of their quality. On the other hand, more attention has been paid to the health and safety of workplaces as policymakers have struggled to contain the spread of the coronavirus. The pay of frontline workers who have continued to provide essential services throughout the crisis has also been the focus of attention. These 'minimum wage heroes' include those working in health and social care, delivery services, food production, and retail sales.

Of particular relevance to this book is the pandemic-induced growth of homeworking and its impact upon the job quality of those involved and, in turn, their well-being. This chapter draws on both historical and contemporary evidence to assess what impact homeworking and remote working, more broadly, can have on: work–life balance; the intensity of work; promotion and development opportunities; health and safety; and, ultimately, employee well-being. It also considers some of the policy responses aimed to help employees draw a clearer boundary between work and home, and make working at home a permanent option that employees can choose in the future.

5.2 Work–Life Balance

The defining characteristic of working at home is that working life and home life directly overlap (cf. Chapter 2). The lived experience of these individuals is therefore shaped, on the one hand, by spatial proximity to the domestic life of the household and, on the other, by geographical distance from co-workers located elsewhere in the organisation. These dual characteristics pose distinctive dilemmas, challenges, and opportunities for maintaining work–life balance (Clark, 2000). These issues are not faced by workers whose working lives and home lives take place in spatially distinct and separate environments. These workers can leave the office or factory and go home; this is not an option for those working at home whose journey to and from work is a matter of steps, if that. The difficulty of drawing a boundary between work and home represents a particular challenge for these workers as the quotes at the beginning of this chapter illustrate.

Media stories frequently portray working at home as a way of allowing mothers, in particular, to care for their children and engage in paid work at the same time and in the same place (see Mirchandani, 2000: 160–162 for examples). However, the home can be a problematic workplace in which to juggle these two roles successfully. Spatial and temporal borders need to be agreed and maintained whenever work takes place at home (Bulos and Chaker,

1995; Ahrentzen, 1990, 1992; Tietze and Musson, 2002). This is not an easy undertaking.

Even when agreed, spatial borders between domestic activities and those devoted to work can shift over time. This may depend on the domestic activities taking place in the home or who is present. Desks, tables, computers, and rooms that are allocated to work activities between certain hours may be reclaimed by other members of the household for non-work purposes, such as homework, playing games, emailing friends, or browsing the Internet. Although there may be a general understanding about the scheduling and duration of working hours, other household members may shift their expectations when minor or major domestic crises develop, such as burst water pipes or a sick child. Some working times may be permissible, others negotiable, and yet others out of the question. The relative acceptability of these time slots is shaped by the work timetables of others and the domestic arrangements of the household.

Nevertheless, the literature suggests that two contrasting approaches are adopted by those working at home (Miraftab, 1996; Shamir, 1992; Beach, 1989; Christensen, 1995). One approach is to cut off where work is carried out from the rest of the household. In this situation, there are clear spatial boundaries between areas dedicated to different purposes, thereby replicating the conventional divisions of home and work under one roof. Before the pandemic, organisations with flexible working policies often insisted that those working at home had a separate space or at least one which offered security and privacy (ACAS, 2014). The other approach is to fuse the two activities, thereby integrating workstations into domestic life. In these circumstances, it is not possible to identify a boundary between locations devoted to work and non-work activities. These options are summed up by one of the respondents to a Swedish study carried out in the mid-1990s:

> There are two models, one is to integrate the job with the dwelling and then I think the furniture must be subordinated to the home. The other one is, like some people do, to establish a real office at home. It's like opening the door to the working-room and then at once one is at work, in a completely different environment. Those are the alternatives.
>
> (Michelson and Lindén, 1997: 16)

Subsequent research has suggested that such a two-way classification does not capture the complexity of how those working at home organise space. Instead, they suggest a continuum stretching from strict separation through to the integration of domestic and working space (Felstead *et al.*, 2005; Magee, 2000; Nippert-Eng, 1996). Some of the evidence for this argument is based on visual assessments of respondents' workspaces taken by researchers following home-based interviews. Felstead *et al.* (2004), for example, took 245 such colour photographs. These were taken from different angles and designed to reveal the location of the workstations used in the home.

Positions along the continuum include spatial arrangements where work is demarcated from, but within close proximity to, domestic arrangements – referred to as 'juxtaposition'. A good example is a desk located in a room used for other purposes, such as the corner of a bedroom. Another arrangement is where workstations are invisible some, but not all, of the time. Examples here include clearing away all signs of work at the end of each working day or overlaying workstations with domestic decoration that camouflages their real purpose – an arrangement labelled 'assimilation'. There are also cases where domesticity and employment compete for space with neither winning out. These are referred to as spaces of 'collision'. Examples here include spaces that have both work and home paraphernalia and are accessible at all times to the whole family.

There are gender differences in the way working space is organised in the home (Salmi, 1997; Ahrentzen, 1992; Haddon and Silverstone, 1993; Haddon and Lewis, 1994; Sullivan, 2000). For example, the evidence suggests that women who work at home are less likely than men to work in a separate room. Detachment and separation is, therefore, a gendered option. According to a survey of over 1,300 individuals who were working at home in the summer of 2020, women were less likely than men to be working in a room detached from the domestic environment. Furthermore, the same survey also revealed that this spatial arrangement had a statistically significant bearing on the ability of those involved to balance their work and non-work lives. Those who were able to detach themselves spatially from domestic life reported that their lives were better balanced than those who were not able to do so (Marks *et al.*, 2020; Skountridaki *et al.*, 2020).

The type of work done at home and the level of household resources can also influence how well or otherwise individuals can keep the worlds of work and non-work in balance (Crosbie and Moore, 2004). For example, many of those doing manufacturing jobs at home – such as sewing machinists and Christmas cracker makers – do not have a dedicated room in which to work. Moreover, this group of homeworkers tends to be women who often find it difficult to get work, but need the money. When they do get work, the lack of affordable childcare means that they have to work while also looking after the children (cf. Chapter 2). This is in stark contrast to those working in professional jobs who are more likely to live in large houses, have a dedicated space in which to work, and can afford to have their children cared for elsewhere (Moore, 2006). The impact that working at home has on work–life balance varies accordingly.

The home is also gendered in terms of who does what within it (Warren, 2021; Hochschild, 1989). For women, the home is often a place of unpaid work, especially with respect to nurturing, caring, and the delivery of emotional labour. Women retain major responsibility for this kind of work and, in particular, routine tasks such as cleaning, washing, and looking after the children. Meanwhile, men 'help out' by taking on tasks such as gardening and DIY. In June 2020, for example, 70% of employed women in cohabiting couples said that they were mostly responsible for the washing and ironing, 61% the cleaning, 56% the cooking, and 53% the shopping (Warren *et al.*, 2021). Studies also suggest that homeworking makes the situation even more unequal; mothers who work at home take on more housework and childcare, while the same is not true of fathers (e.g. Kim, 2020; Kurowska, 2020).

Evidence is emerging, however, that the dramatic shift of work into the home during the pandemic may be having a more equalising effect as many more men and women have been compelled to work at home. For example, an online survey of 1,160 mainly cohabiting couples carried out in May–June 2020 concluded that 'supporting more men to work from home . . . will be a crucial factor in ensuring that the pandemic does not end up exacerbating the existing gender inequalities' (Chung *et al.*, 2020a: 25, 2020b). It found that fathers who were working at home in the pandemic were significantly more likely to say that they were doing more domestic labour. They were spending more time looking after their children, playing and entertaining them, and cooking for the family during the lockdown than before. Mothers also confirmed that their partners were doing more routine childcare. However, mothers who were already working at home before the pandemic took on an even larger share of the cleaning and childcare duties. So, while the gender imbalance in the domestic division of labour may be weakened where homeworking is new, it may be strengthened where paid work has been regularly carried out at home.

The impact that working at home has on work–life balance can also depend on whether it is an established pattern of working or an informal arrangement that crops up from time to time. Evidence from Finland collected before the pandemic suggests that the latter is more disruptive to family life. Results based on two surveys – each with around 4,000 workers and carried out by Statistics Finland – show that conflicts about household chores, working time, and leisure time are significantly more likely to arise when work tasks are brought home on an ad hoc basis

(Ojala *et al.*, 2014). These instances are unplanned and more disruptive to family life than regular working at home arrangements. For this reason, many workers initially found the shift to working at home during the pandemic a shock to family life. But many got used to it and would like to continue working at home when social distancing restrictions are fully lifted (see Chapter 6).

5.3 Intensity of Work

Nevertheless, whatever the circumstances, it is difficult to achieve a 'good functioning of work and home, with a minimum of role conflict' when the worlds of work and home are intentionally blurred (Clark, 2000: 751). As a result, the pressures of homeworking may spill over into non-work life with workers reporting an inability to 'switch off', difficulty in unwinding when 'off work', and an extension to the working day. They may also report greater work intensity with more effort expended in each hour worked with reduced 'buffer' time between tasks. For example, Zoom meetings scheduled end-on-end with little, if any, breaks in between calls.

Maintaining or even increasing output may come at a cost to employees. For example, a study of information technology professionals who worked at home because of the pandemic showed that they maintained their output by working longer hours and so actual productivity fell (see Chapter 4). This extra unpaid time was spent communicating with colleagues online, an activity which previously they would have done incidentally through encounters in the office (Gibbs *et al.*, 2021). On the other hand, by working more intensively, call centre workers who worked at home recorded higher levels of productivity than their office-based counterparts (Bloom *et al.*, 2015). They spent longer logged onto the system because they took fewer paid breaks. This meant that the working day was less porous; that is, paid periods of on-the-job inactivity – or breathing spaces – between tasks were shorter. Those working at home also dealt with more calls per minute because the home was relatively quiet and free from disturbances. In both cases, the work was more intense.

This may also extend to workers who work remotely, that is, away from the employer's premises and not in direct physical sight of management. A British study based on pooling several Skills and Employment Surveys broadened this definition a step further by including those who worked mainly as well as partly away from the premises of the employer (Felstead and Henseke, 2017). This definition, then, captures those who work anywhere outside the employer's premises for at least one day a week. These locations include the home, but also the local café, public library, co-working spaces, shared offices, or while on the move (cf. Chapter 2).

The study found that significantly greater proportions of such workers strongly agreed that their job required them to work very hard, that they worked beyond formal working hours to get the job done, and that they put in more effort than was required. For example, 39.9% of remote workers said that it was 'very true' that 'I often have to work extra time, over and above the formal hours of my job, to get through the work or to help out' compared to 24.1% of those in conventional workplaces. These differences were confirmed by regression analyses which took into account the contrasting composition of the two groups in terms of occupation, industry, educational level, and household composition. These results suggest that the work effort expended by remote workers was significantly higher than otherwise identical fixed-place workers. This supports qualitative research which suggests that work effort is higher among remote workers (Kelliher and Anderson, 2011). The Felstead and Henseke (2017) study suggests that the working day of remote workers is longer, the intensity of each hour worked is higher, and more voluntary effort is expended.

Remote workers also found it more difficult to reconcile home and work life. They found it harder to unwind and more often reported worrying about work at the end of the working day. Around a third (36.0%) of conventionally sited workers kept worrying about job problems at least some of the time even when they were not working, but among remote workers the proportion was eight percentage points higher. Again, this difference remains even when compared to otherwise identical workers who operated in single fixed places of work. These results underline the downside of remote working suggested by border theory with workers finding it difficult to separate their work and non-work lives (Clark, 2000).

A similar picture is confirmed by the Living, Work and Covid-19 Survey which collected data on around 87,000 people living and working in the European Union in the period April–July 2020 (excluding the UK). The survey shows that employees working at home were more likely to report that: at least sometimes they did not 'have enough time to get the job done'; they were 'emotionally drained by work' most or all of the time; and they felt isolated most or all of the time. They were also less likely to think that they were doing a useful job than those who did not work at home (Eurofound, 2020b: 35–43). In addition, those working at home because of the Covid-19 pandemic were more likely to report that their working hours had increased and that they had to work in their free time to get things done (see Figure 5.1). This suggests that working at home has prompted an extension to the working day and that working hours have also become more intense.

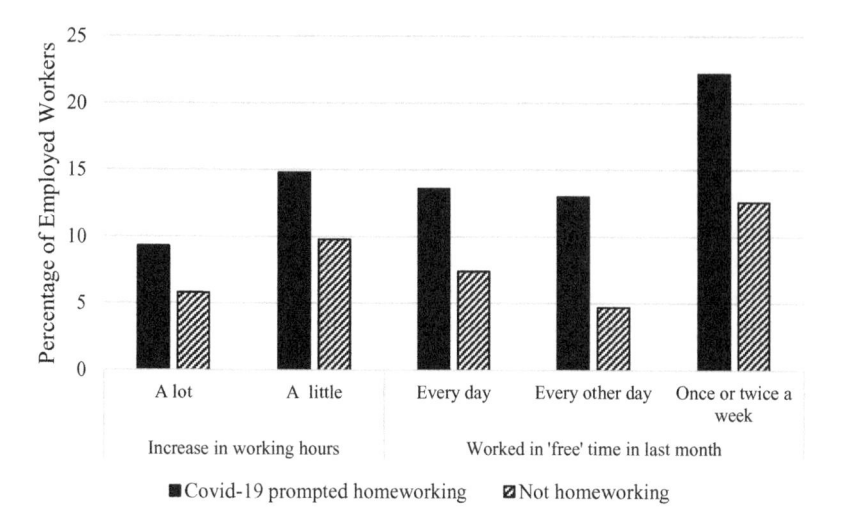

Figure 5.1 Paid and Unpaid Working Hours by Location of Work, European Union, April 2020

Source: Own calculations from Eurofound's Living, Working and Covid-19 Survey, April 2020 (excluding the UK because of Brexit), see Eurofound (2020a).

Other studies carried out during the pandemic have also revealed the growing intensity of work and the difficulties employees face in disconnecting from working life (see Prospect, 2021). They show that

- UK employees, on average, worked an extra 2.5 hours a day when they worked at home compared to what they were doing before the pandemic began (Meakin, 2021).
- Over a third of homeworkers in the US were substituting their commuting time for long hours of work (Barrero *et al.*, 2020).
- In the UK, homeworkers were spending more of their time working in the evening, that is, hours of the day when they would have previously commuted. They were also doing more unpaid work: in 2020, they did 6.0 hours of unpaid overtime on average per week compared to 3.6 hours if they worked in an office or factory (Martin *et al.*, 2021).
- Connection time with work has increased; the gap between the first and last email of the day rose by almost 50 minutes according to a cross-country study carried out eight weeks on either side of the start of the pandemic (i.e. mid-March 2020 (DeFilippis *et al.*, 2020).

- When asked to evaluate what effect working at home as opposed to the office had on their experience of work, survey respondents reported that working at home was more intense; homeworkers were three times more likely to report doing more work, operating under greater pressure and working at a faster pace (Taylor *et al.*, 2021).
- Video conferencing is being used more frequently outside of office hours – early in the morning, in the evening, and over the weekend (Spataro, 2020).
- There has been an explosion of email communication which adds to the intensity of the working day (Microsoft, 2021).
- During the pandemic, 44% of employees in the UK said that they could never fully 'switch off' from work (Aviva, 2020).
- Over half (56%) of those who had switched to homeworking during the pandemic in the UK, said they had found it harder to 'switch off' as a result (Royal Society for Public Health, 2021).
- Work-related stress rose. This was prompted, in part, by out-of-hours demands and requests, such as a woman who 'complained of a supervisor sending nine-page memos on Sunday nights, making it difficult for her to sleep' (Jacobs and Warwick-Ching, 2021).
- Work intensity and stress levels increased for the majority of those who switched to working at home, according to an Irish survey. A sizeable minority of these switchers (44%) said that they felt under pressure to answer telephone calls and emails outside of working hours (Financial Services Union, 2020).

Circumstances where employees feel that they need to be available all the time to answer emails, calls, or simply deal with rising workloads are known as the 'availability creep' (Pocock, 2021). This 'always on' culture is not a new phenomenon. However, it is one that has been accelerated by the shift to homeworking and difficulties of drawing and maintaining temporal boundaries around work as the evidence presented earlier testifies. This has intensified interest in initiatives designed to give employees the 'right to disconnect'.

Initiatives to halt the availability creep have been taken across Europe well before the pandemic began. Sometimes these have been taken by individual companies, have formed part of collective agreements with trade unions and/or found their way into government action or even legislation. Some companies have taken unilateral action to help employees draw the line between home and work; for example, by encouraging or stopping employees from sending emails to each other when they are off-shift and/or on holiday. Ever since 2013, Renault discouraged its staff across the world from sending emails in the evening and at weekends. Some employers have gone a step further by taking action to disconnect employees and so preventing them from working outside of their stipulated hours. In 2012, Volkswagen configured its company servers to ensure that emails could not be sent and received 30 minutes after employees stop work and 30 minutes before they return. In much the same spirit, Daimler introduced a policy in 2014 which set employees' email inboxes to 'holiday mode' when they were on annual leave. The software automatically deletes all incoming emails during that period. Senders receive an auto-response stating that during the employee's period of leave emails will be deleted. They are offered an alternative employee to contact. The policy applies to all employees who have a company email address; hence, it covers around half of the workforce (Vargas-Llave *et al.*, 2020).

In other cases, these arrangements have been suggested by, and then agreed with, the relevant trade unions. For example, as part of a company-level agreement signed in 2014, those working remotely for BMW are encouraged to agree fixed 'times of reachability' with their supervisors. All employees, remote or otherwise, are also allowed to register time spent working outside of the employers' premises as working time, hence allowing employees to get paid for working outside of their regular hours. Collective agreements are also in place for those working for Orange in France and Telefónica in Italy who can refuse to respond to 'out of hours' emails and telephone calls without detriment (Messenger *et al.*, 2017). Sector-level agreements are also in place across certain sectors in Europe, such as the oil sector in France.

National governments across Europe, too, have taken action. To varying degrees, there is a legal right to disconnect in France, Belgium, Spain, and Italy (Vargas-Llave *et al.*, 2020: 41). Sparked by the pandemic, legislative intervention is also under discussion in the European Parliament and in many individual member states. Ireland has been the quickest to act. As of 1 April 2021, employees have the right to switch off from work outside normal working hours. This includes the right not to respond immediately to emails, telephone calls, or other messages. They cannot be penalised for doing so and are required to respect the working hours of others by not emailing or calling colleagues outside of normal working hours. The Irish Government is also consulting on plans to make it easier for employees to work off the employers' premises well after the pandemic has ended. These actions form part of its national strategy of promoting remote working (Government of Ireland, 2021).

However, there is no specific legislation in the UK that allows workers to disconnect. There is no positive right that enables employees to carve out 'communication free' time when they cannot be contacted by management and/or work colleagues (Allen and Masters, 2021). Instead, there are laws that set minimum rest periods during the working day, minimum levels of holiday leave, and a cap is set on the number of hours worked per week (although this is subject to an opt-out). This lack of protection has led to calls by trade unions and opposition parties for employees to be given greater protection and hence halt turning homes into '24/7 offices'. Whether such a right is included in the forthcoming Employment Bill – promised in the Queen's Speech in 2019 – or in any future employment legislation, only time will tell.

5.4 Promotion and Development Opportunities

One of the downsides often reported by employees is the fear that while off-site, they are 'out of sight and out of mind'. They are therefore passed over for promotion and have fewer opportunities to develop their skills and experience as a result of 'proximity bias'. Newcomers, in particular, may suffer most from the increased geographical dispersion of workers since it makes their induction into a community of practitioners more difficult (Jewson, 2008). Physical proximity with co-workers facilitates serendipitous contacts and promotes non-verbal communication through body language, eye contact, and touching rituals such as the handshake. It also allows unintentional, on-the-job learning to take place and increases face time with line managers and colleagues.

Evidence suggests that these fears are real. For example, Bloom *et al.* (2015: 205–207) examined the career trajectories of two groups of employees who volunteered to take part in an experiment to examine the effects of working at home. Volunteers were randomly divided into two groups – a treatment group that was kitted out to work at home and a control group that remained office-based during the experiment. Promotion data for around 125 employees in each group were collected over a 22-month period. For this study, promotion was defined as either being made team leader who line managed a group of 10–15 operators or being given a more advanced role in the team in readiness for promotion to team leader. A total of 17 employees who worked at home gained promotion during the experiment compared to 23 of those who were office-based.

However, these simple counts do not take into account differences between the two groups such as job tenure, education level, and, importantly, performance. When factored in, the regression results show that working at home had both negative and positive effects on the chances of promotion. On the one hand, working at home improved performance levels (such as the number of calls handled and the length of time available) and hence raised the chances of promotion. On the other hand, working at home reduced the chances of promotion since managers were less aware of the superior performance levels of off-site workers and were less likely to promote them as a result. Working at home may also make it difficult for employees to develop the interpersonal skills needed to become a team leader. Their function is to liaise with members of the team, help resolve problems, provide ongoing training, and improve operator performance while patrolling the area occupied by the team. These skills are difficult to develop while sitting at home, physically and aurally detached from the team they are subsequently expected to lead.

Those working at home across a variety of jobs and in a range of industries are similarly disadvantaged. Using official data collected in the UK, researchers have followed the fortunes of several cohorts of workers across a 15-month period between 2011 and 2017 (Martin *et al.*, 2021). During each of these periods, the same individuals were questioned about where they worked, and whether they had been given additional managerial responsibilities, received a pay rise, and/or undertaken training. Promotion is defined as individuals who gained managerial/supervisory responsibilities or received a substantial pay rise (30% or more) during the 15 months they were studied. The results show that by doing most of their work at home an individual's chances of promotion was halved, even after holding all other factors constant. Some of these factors might themselves be associated with promotion – for example, the chances of promotion fall as individuals get older. Similarly, those who transitioned over the 15-month period from doing most of their work away from the home to a position where they worked mostly at home saw their chances of promotion almost halved.

Conversely, when a worker moved the other way – from homeworking towards office-based working – their chances of promotion improved. This left them just as likely to be promoted as their office-based counterparts. In other words, the disadvantage of homeworking did not linger beyond the time they spent off-site. These findings do, however, suggest that home-workers may be overlooked for promotion due to the lack of face-to-face interaction with colleagues and/or superiors.

The same study also suggests that those working mainly at home were less likely to receive job-related training; they were 40% less likely to do so than those who did not work at home at all. Nevertheless, this disadvantage started to fall in 2020 when, of course, working at home became more widespread as offices were closed and more activities, including training, moved online. However, we know relatively little about whether the penalty of homeworking in terms of career progression and skill development will persist in the future. Qualitative evidence suggests that it has been detrimental to some, especially women who have generally shouldered the greatest domestic burden. Eva – a university lecturer in the UK – for example, said that she had to give up research work as soon as the pandemic began:

> My children were at home with me and something had to give and it wasn't going to be the teaching. The only person who is affected by me not doing research is me, not my employer. A year's setback on my research is detrimental for my personal career.
>
> (quoted in Jacobs and Warwick-Ching, 2021)

Moreover, as the pandemic recedes and as a mixture of homeworking and office working becomes more common, it is unknown what effect this will have on the promotion prospects and development opportunities for those involved. This is a feature of job quality that will need to be monitored and assessed. The fear is that those who have greatest to gain from rubbing shoulders with and being in the physical presence of others – such as new recruits – may lose out in a post-pandemic world where remote working is more common.

5.5 Health and Safety

Under the *Health and Safety at Work Act (HSWA) 1974*, employers have a duty under law to ensure, as far as is reasonably practical, the health and safety of their employees at work. Since individual workers are ill-placed to acquire full information about an employers' health and safety record and to calculate the risks associated with the work, the Health and Safety Executive (HSE) was set up to do so on workers' behalf. When originally conceived, the 'duty of care' undertaking was drafted with the physical well-being of the worker in mind, but it has since broadened to include mental well-being.

The widespread use of ICT now means that employers have to protect employees from the health risks of working with display screen equipment (DSE), such as PCs, laptops, tablets, and smartphones. The *Health and Safety (Display Screen Equipment) Regulations 1992* apply to employees who use DSE daily, for an hour or more at a time. To comply, risk assessments of each employee's workstation need to be carried out. For each workstation, a checklist needs to be completed by the employee with follow-up help and support given if required. The list also includes advice about posture, screen positioning, and proper use of equipment. These regulations apply to all employees whether they are working on the employer's premises or not.

However, adherence to these regulations tends to be lower when workers are working at home. According to an online survey of over 3,000 employees, for example, checks on the health and safety of workstations were less frequent when individuals worked at home. Set-ups associated with musculoskeletal injuries – such as desk height, positioning of chair, sitting posture, and screen glare – were between 5 and 15 percentage points less frequently checked when individuals worked at home than when they were in the office. Not surprisingly, therefore, large proportions of respondents complained of an increase in musculoskeletal difficulties as a result of homeworking: stiff shoulders (41.7%); stiff neck (40.6%); backache (39.4%); and pain or numbness in hands, wrists, or arms (23.6%) (Taylor *et al.*, 2021). Some of this may be due to the lack of space available to homeworkers. One survey suggests that in 2020 over one in four people (26%) were working either on a sofa or in a bedroom used at other times by themselves or their children. Those doing so were more likely to report the type of musculoskeletal difficulties outlined earlier (RSPH, 2021).

Working at home may also have heightened the tendency for workers to work while ill. While out of sight, workers have fewer ways of demonstrating their commitment to the organisation. They cannot make themselves visible by arriving early in the office and leaving late or by symbolically leaving personal possessions – coats, jackets, and bags – on the desk when in the office, but elsewhere in the building. However, they can more easily work at home when ill since they no longer have to commute and be present in the office. This tendency was evident before the pandemic when homeworking was relatively low.

A pre-pandemic study of call centre operators, referred to earlier, showed that those who worked at home took fewer sick days than their office-based counterparts. When questioned operators put this down to the fact that even when ill they would continue to work at home, whereas they would take sick leave if they had to come into the office to do the work (Bloom *et al.*, 2015: 191–192). Recent evidence, too, suggests that working while ill is widespread among homeworkers of all types. Almost two-thirds (63.5%) of homeworkers surveyed during the pandemic said that they carried on working even when they were unwell and should not have been working (Taylor *et al.*, 2021).

The instruction to work at home has also led to the dramatic increase in the use of videoconferencing through a variety of platforms such as Teams, Google Meet, Webex, and Zoom. The latter, in particular, has helped millions of people to connect with others. It is free to use for short video calls and is easy to install. The Zoom software was downloaded nearly 500 million times in 2020, up from 16 million downloads the year before. Its popularity peaked in April 2020 when it was downloaded 3.5 million times in a single day. It has, therefore, become a ubiquitous tool that many of us now use daily. This is reflected in the common use of the word 'Zoom' as a verb to replace videoconferencing in much the same way as we use 'Googling' to refer to searching the Internet.

While videoconferencing has greatly facilitated working at home, its use can be exhausting. This has become known as 'Zoom fatigue' and stems from the psychological challenges of using the videoconferencing interface instead of sitting in face-to-face meetings. While the brand name Zoom is used in this emerging debate, the issues apply to other videoconferencing platforms.

First, unlike face-to-face meetings, everyone on a Zoom call is visible to each other regardless of who is speaking. Also, everyone has eye contact with everyone on the call, provided all callers have their cameras on, and they are looking into the lens and are not looking away. Compare this with a face-to-face meeting, where each person speaks. While they are speaking, listeners turn to face the speaker and when others speak they are looked at instead. It is rare for a listener to stare at another listener throughout the meeting. Yet, all participants in a Zoom meeting are stared at all of the time. As Bailenson (2021: 5) puts it: 'from a perceptual standpoint, Zoom effectively transforms listeners into speakers and smoothers everyone with eye gaze'. The meeting, therefore, becomes more intense given that everyone is visible to everyone else all of the time ensuring that there is no escape from the gaze of others.

Secondly, on Zoom users need to work harder to send and receive non-verbal signals. Examples of sending non-verbal cues include arranging the background that viewers see, looking directly into the camera, using hand movements, nodding, or shaking the head to signal approval or disapproval, moving closer to the camera, and speaking louder. Another source of cognitive load is receiving cues from others. This is particularly difficult on a videoconference call since head and eye movements cannot be directed at one particular individual, but are instead broadcast to all. Even keeping track of where individuals appear on screen can be difficult as callers often do not have the same grid layout. Gestures and glances between participants are not possible, but they are common in face-to-face meetings. During one-to-one calls, some of these difficulties can be overcome and the encounter can become less intense as a result. Although even here callers are made visible to each other and so they have to perform accordingly. During telephone calls, on the other hand, callers rely wholly on verbal cues and signals, and do not have to bother about how they look like, how they are dressed, or even what they are doing while on the call.

Thirdly, the default setting for Zoom is that participants see their own real-time camera feed while on the call. On other platforms, the camera feed may be smaller than it is for Zoom, but it is there nevertheless. Users, therefore, see a reflection of themselves, while having a conversation with others. It is suggested that this may have a larger detrimental effect on women who are forced to look at themselves while at work, and may be more critical of their own body image and the way they look.

Lastly, cameras have a limited field of vision. This means that Zoom users typically sit between a half and one metre away from the camera (typically located on the top of a laptop or desktop monitor). Users usually position themselves in the centre of the screen by altering the angle of the camera and ensuring that their faces can be seen. This limits their physical mobility. Unlike face-to-face meetings, those on a Zoom call cannot stand up, move around, go to the water cooler and get up to use the flipchart. Furthermore, the use of Zoom also allows more meetings to be held with minimal breaks in between calls. Face-to-face meetings, on the other hand, are unlikely to be held end-on-end and may even take place in different parts of the building or even in different cities. This can involve short bursts of moderate exercise – such as cycling or walking to and from meetings – and provide 'buffer' time for workers to recompose and prepare themselves for the next bout of work activity.

Given the benefits of videoconferencing – its ease, reach, and efficiency – its use is likely to outlast the pandemic and be with us for decades to come. That said, its use does raise important issues for health and safety which, like many other themes covered in this book, will no doubt form the basis of future research on remote working.

5.6 Employee Well-being

Studies of job quality have focused on the objective features of work that have the capability of enhancing or diminishing employee well-being (e.g. Felstead *et al.*, 2019; Green, 2006). These include enabling employees to balance work and non-work commitments, not putting them under undue pressure, offering promotion and development opportunities, and protecting their health and safety. Working at home has impacts on all these objective features of work – sometimes for the better, sometimes for the worse. In turn, these can diminish or improve employee well-being.

Rather than trace each of the links in this chain, some researchers have examined the direct association that the location of work has with employee well-being. Job satisfaction is often used as the best available proxy for the latter. This indicator typically takes one of two forms in surveys. Either it is based on employees' overall assessment of their jobs. Or it is an averaged evaluation of different aspects of the job given by each employee. For both indicators, respondents are given a seven- or five-point scale from which to choose. Satisfaction with particular aspects of the job – such as pay and hours of work – have also been investigated along with non-work life – such as the amount of leisure time.

The results of this research suggest that homeworking is associated with higher levels of job satisfaction when compared to those with similar characteristics who do not work at home. This finding is based on data taken from large cross-sectional and longitudinal surveys (e.g. Wheatley, 2012, 2016; Reuschke, 2019) and smaller scale comparison studies of employees working in different locations (e.g. Fonner and Roloff, 2010). However, studies also suggest that the positive effects of homeworking level off the more time people spend working at home (Golden and Veiga, 2005). Furthermore, qualitative studies suggest that the strength of this association depends on whether working at home is an arrangement requested by employees or an arrangement thrust upon employees by employers (e.g. Kelliher and Anderson, 2011; Harris, 2003).

Focusing on job satisfaction has undoubted advantages. First and foremost, it is widely available in many data sets. Secondly, there are good reasons for collecting data on employees' feelings about their job. Higher levels of job dissatisfaction, for example, are often a precursor to employees quitting and moving on. Thirdly, focusing on job satisfaction avoids having to specify in advance what really matters in a job – if workers are happy with their lot, however small or large, then that is good enough.

However, focusing on job satisfaction as the only measure of employee well-being is problematic. Its biggest drawback is that satisfaction ratings are reflective of each employee's individual preferences and expectations with the same objective job features evaluated differently from employee to employee. What one employee feels about a job may differ from the feelings of another. Employees' satisfaction levels vary according to demographic differences such as gender, ethnicity, region, and age. For example, research has shown that women are more satisfied with their jobs than men, lowly paid workers are just as satisfied with their jobs as those who are highly paid, and job satisfaction falls and then rises with age (Clark, 1997; Brown *et al.*, 2007; Clark *et al.*, 1996).

Despite these criticisms, other proxies also suggest that off-site working boosts well-being. Evidence from the Skills and Employment Survey, for example, suggests those who work remotely – that is off-site for at least one day a week – are more positively inclined towards the employer. Seven out of ten remote workers agreed or strongly agreed that they would not move to another organisation for higher pay compared to around six out of ten conventionally sited workers. A similar pattern is repeated for other organisational commitment style questions from which an index can be created. Regression analysis of that index shows that, all other things being equal, organisational commitment is significantly higher for those who work remotely. Furthermore, remote workers report that their jobs are significantly more pleasurable and stimulating (Felstead and Henseke, 2017).

However, the sudden and dramatic movement of work into the home as a result of the pandemic might be expected to have had a damaging effect on employee well-being. After all, previous evidence suggests that forced homeworking can be detrimental to well-being. Furthermore, the isolation of working exclusively working at home with little face-to-face contact with others can raise anxiety levels in particular (Wood *et al.*, 2021).

There is evidence that at the start of the pandemic these forces may have been strong, hence putting downward pressure on the mental health of employees who were suddenly told to work exclusively at home. For example, over 30% of those working always or often at home in June 2020 – the third month of the spring lockdown in the UK – reported that they were able to concentrate less or much less than usual compared to less than 20% of those who reported that they had not worked at home at all. Similarly, those who worked mainly at home – always or often – reported greater difficulties in enjoying normal day-to-day activities and more often felt constantly being under strain and unhappy with life. Furthermore, multivariate analysis shows that those who were exclusively working at home during April and May 2020 had significantly lower levels of mental health overall than those who did not work at home at all. However, by June the fall was not as steep and not statistically significant from other workers. This may be because those working at home became more accustomed to working in this way and/or those who found it difficult to do so had voted with their feet and moved back to the office (Felstead and Reuschke, 2020: 14–16). The findings also suggest that mental health declined significantly among those who reported that they were not as productive while working at home (Etheridge *et al.*, 2020).

This evidence gives empirical support to those who argue that working at home should be a day one employment right. Giving all employees the opportunity to vary their location of work can have business and individual benefits when it is offered as a choice open to all. However, during the pandemic, employees were given little option but to work at home or lose their job. Before that, the right to request flexible working was gradually being extended to more employees. When it was first introduced in 2003, it was only available to parents of young children. It was extended to carers in 2007 and to parents of older children in 2009. Then, in 2014, all employees with at least 26 weeks' continuous employment were given the right to request a change in hours, times, or location of work (Kelliher and de Menezes, 2019). The sudden switch to working at home prompted by the pandemic has prompted the UK Government to consider dropping the qualifying period to be dropped altogether and for the right to request flexible working to become a day one right (BEIS, 2021). Existing evidence suggests that the decision to work at home or not is likely to be beneficial to both employees and employers, but these are issues that will need to be corroborated and tracked in the years ahead.

5.7 Conclusion

Before the pandemic, job quality was a hot topic. While it remains of significant policy interest today, attention has inevitably focused on the post-pandemic recovery and the protection of jobs. The effects of homeworking for employers and employees in these debates loom large.

One of the biggest challenges homeworkers face is how to mentally 'switch on and off', and how to arrange the available space within the home. This involves the creation of boundaries between two spheres of social life that have traditionally been spatially divided. More time spent at home can also have knock-on effects on the domestic division of labour. Some household tasks, such as putting the washing machine on, for example, can be done in between bouts of work and time saved from the daily commute may be used to cook or tidy up.

The blurring of boundaries can also lead to a more intensive working environment with fewer interruptions and more time spent on the job. Working hours, too, may be extended with no natural end to the working day. Previously, this end point might have been set by knowing when to leave the office in order to miss the worst of the rush-hour traffic or to catch a particular train to get home.

Working at home can also be detrimental to an employee's chances of promotion and access to training opportunities. In addition, the workstations used by homeworkers may not be as safe as those in offices where standard equipment such as desks, chairs, keyboards, and screens are provided and are well maintained.

Despite these drawbacks, employees' who work at home report high levels of job satisfaction and appear to enjoy working at home. However, we know very little about the effect that homeworking has on other aspects of job quality such as job security, involvement in decision-making, and its long-term impact on skill and pay levels. Furthermore, the evidence on which this chapter draws was either carried out before the pandemic, when homeworking was less prevalent, or during the pandemic, when many employees were forced to work entirely at home. We, therefore, know less about the effect that different working arrangements can have on employee well-being and many of the antecedents reviewed in this chapter. This includes working in a variety of places or allowing employees to 'pick and mix' where they work, referred to as remote and hybrid working, respectively. Yet, as the following chapter goes on to argue, it is these working arrangements that are likely to characterise the 'new normal' as the pandemic recedes and restrictions on social mixing are lifted once and for all.

References

ACAS (2014) *Homeworking – A Guide for Employers and Employees*, London: Advisory, Conciliation and Arbitration Service.

Ahrentzen, S (1990) 'Managing conflict by managing boundaries: how professional homeworkers cope with multiple roles at home', *Environment and Behaviour*, 22(6): 723–752.

Ahrentzen, S (1992) 'Home as a workplace in the lives of women', in Altman, I and Low, S (eds) *Place Attachment*, London: Plenum Press.

Allen, R and Masters, D (2021) *Technology Managing People – The Legal Implications*, London: Trades Union Congress.

Aviva (2020) *Embracing the Age of Ambiguity: Re-Invigorating the Workforce in a Rapidly Evolving World*, York: Aviva.

Bailenson, J N (2021) 'Nonverbal overload: a theoretical argument for the causes of zoom fatigue', *Technology, Mind and Behavior*, 1(3): 1–13.

Barrero, J, Bloom, N and Davis, S J (2020) *60 Million Fewer Commuting Hours Per Day: How Americans Use Time Saved by Working from Home*, Becker Friedman Institute Working Paper, No. 132, Chicago: Becker Friedman Institute.

Beach, B (1989) *Integrating Work and Family Life: The Home-Working Family*, New York: State University of New York Press.

BEIS (2021) *Making Flexible Working the Default*, London: Department for Business, Energy and Industrial Strategy.

Bloom, N, Liang, J, Roberts, J and Ying, Z J (2015) 'Does working from home work? Evidence from a Chinese experiment', *Quarterly Journal of Economics*, 130(1): 165–218.

Brown, A, Charlwood, A, Forde, C and Spencer, D (2007) 'Job quality and the economics of new labour: a critical appraisal using subjective survey data', *Cambridge Journal of Economics*, 31(6): 941–971.

Bulos, M and Chaker, W (1995) 'Sustaining a sense of home and personal identity', in Benjamin, D and Stea, D (eds) *The Home: Words, Interpretations, Meanings and Environments*, Aldershot: Avebury.

Christensen, K (1995) *Impacts of Computer-Mediated Home-Based Work on Women and Their Families*, New York: Center for Human Environments.

Chung, H, Birkett, H Forbes, S and Seo, H (2020a) 'Working from home and the division of housework and childcare among dual earner couples during the pandemic in the UK', *SocioArxiv*: 1–23, December.

Chung, H, Seo, H, Forbes, S and Birkett, H (2020b) *Working from Home During the COVID-19 Lockdown: Changing Preferences and the Future of Work*, Canterbury: University of Kent.

Clark, A (1997) 'Job satisfaction and gender: why are women so happy at work?', *Labour Economics*, 4: 341–372.

Clark, A, Oswald, A and Warr, P (1996) 'Is job satisfaction U-shaped in age?', *Journal of Occupational and Organizational Psychology*, 69: 57–81.

Clark, S C (2000) 'Work/family border theory: a new theory of work/family balance', *Human Relations*, 53(6): 747–770.

Crosbie, T and Moore, J (2004) 'Work-life balance and working from home', *Social Policy and Society*, 3(3): 223–233.

DeFilippis, E, Impink, S M, Singell, M, Polzer, J T and Sadun, R (2020) *Collaborating During Coronavirus: The Impact of Covid-19 on the Nature of Work*, NBER Working Paper Series, Working Paper, No. 27612, Cambridge, MA: National Bureau of Economic Research.

Etheridge, B, Wang, Y and Tang, L (2020) *Worker Productivity During Lockdown and Working from Home: Evidence from Self-Reports*, Institute for Social and Economic Research, No. 2020–12, Colchester: Institute for Economic and Social Research, University of Essex.

Eurofound (2020a) *Living, Working and COVID-19 Dataset*, Dublin: European Foundation for the Improvement of Living and Working Conditions.

Eurofound (2020b) *Living, Working and COVID-19*, Luxembourg: Publications of the European Union.

European Commission (2001) *Communication from the Commission to the Council, the European Parliament, the European Economic and Social Committee and the Committee of the Regions, Employment and Social Policies: A Framework for Investing in Quality, COM (2001) 313 Final*, Luxembourg: Publications of the Office of the European Union.

Felstead, A, Gallie, D, Green, F and Henseke, G (2019) 'Conceiving, designing and trailing a short form measure of job quality: a proof-of-concept study', *Industrial Relations Journal*, 50(1): 2–19.

Felstead, A and Henseke, G (2017) 'Assessing the growth of remote working and its consequences for effort, well-being and work-life balance', *New Technology, Work and Employment*, 32(3): 195–212.

Felstead, A, Jewson, N and Walters, S (2004) 'Images, interviews and interpretations: making connections in visual research', in Pole, C (ed) *Seeing Is Believing? Approaches to Visual Research*, Oxford: Elsevier Science.

Felstead, A, Jewson, N and Walters, S (2005) *Changing Places of Work*, Basingstoke and New York: Palgrave Macmillan.

Felstead, A and Reuschke, D (2020) *Homeworking in the UK: Before and During the 2020 Lockdown*, WISERD Report, Cardiff: Wales Institute of Social and Economic Research, August.

Financial Services Union (2020) 'Union calls for right to disconnect to "offset the downsides of homeworking"', *FSU News Release*, 26 May, www.fsunion.org/updates/newsreleases/2020/05/26/union-calls-for-right-to-disconnect-to-offset-the/ (accessed 25 July 2021).

Fonner, K L and Roloff, M E (2010) 'Why teleworkers are more satisfied with their jobs than are office-based workers: when less contact is beneficial', *Journal of Applied Communication Research*, 38(4): 336–361.

Gibbs, M, Mengel, F and Siemroth, C (2021) *Work from Home and Productivity: Evidence from Personnel and Analytics Data on IT Professionals*,

Becker Friedman Institute Working Paper, No. 56, Chicago: Becker Friedman Institute.

Golden, T D and Veiga, J F (2005) 'The impact of extent of telecommuting on job satisfaction: resolving inconsistent findings', *Journal of Management*, 31(2): 301–318.

Government of Ireland (2021) *Making Remote Work: National Remote Work Strategy*, Dublin: Department of Enterprise, Trade and Industry.

Green, F (2006) *Demanding Work: The Paradox of Job Quality in the Affluent Economy*, Princeton: Princeton University Press.

Haddon, L and Lewis, A (1994) 'The experience of teleworking: an annotated review', *The International Journal of Human Resource Management*, 5(1): 195–223.

Haddon, L and Silverstone, R (1993) *Teleworking in the 1990s: A View from the Home*, SPRU CICT Report Series, No. 10, Falmer: University of Sussex.

Harris, L (2003) 'Home-based teleworking and the employment relationship', *Personnel Review*, 32(4): 422–437.

Hochschild, A R (1989) *The Second Shift*, New York: Aron Books.

Hurrell, D-L, Hughes, C and Ball, E (2017) *Local Employment Charters: Case Studies from the UK*, Manchester: Inclusive Growth Analysis Unit.

ILO (1999) *Decent Work: International Labour Conference, 87th Session 1999*, Geneva: International Labour Office.

Jacobs, E and Warwick-Ching, L (2021) 'Feeling the strain: stress and anxiety weigh on world's workers', *Financial Times*, 8 February.

Jewson, N (2008) 'Communities of practice in their place: some implications of changes in the spatial location of work', in Hughes, J, Jewson, N and Unwin, L (eds) *Communities of Practice: Critical Perspectives*, London: Routledge.

Kelliher, C and Anderson, D (2011) 'Doing more with less? Flexible working practices and the intensification of work', *Human Relations*, 63(1): 83–106.

Kelliher, C and de Menezes, L M (2019) *Flexible Working in Organisations: A Research Overview*, London: Routledge.

Kim, J (2020) 'Workplace flexibility and parent-child interactions among working parents in the US', *Social Indicators Research*, 151(2): 427–469.

Kurowska, A (2020) 'Gendered effects of home-based work on parents' capability to balance work with non-work: two countries with different models of division of labour compared', *Social Indicators Research*, 151(2): 405–425.

Magee, J L (2000) 'Home as an alternative workplace: negotiating the spatial and behavioural boundaries between home and work', *Journal of Interior Design*, 26(1): 35–47.

Marks, A, Mallett, O, Zschomler and Skountridaki, L (2020) 'Written evidence given to the House of Lords COVID-19 committee', 10 December, www.workingathome.org.uk/wp-content/uploads/2021/01/HofL-final_-working-at-home.pdf (accessed 23 July 2021).

Martin, J, Haigney, V, Lawrence, B and Walton, A (2021) *Homeworking Hours, Rewards and Opportunities in the UK: 2011 to 2020*, Newport: Office for National Statistics.

Meakin, L (2021) 'Remote working's longer hours are new normal for many', *Bloomberg Wealth*, 2 February, www.bloomberg.com/news/articles/2021-02-02/remote-working-s-longer-hours-are-new-normal-for-many-chart (accessed 25 July 2021).

Messenger, J, Vargas-Llave, O, Gschwind, L, Boehmer, S, Vermeylen, G and Wilkens, M (2017) *Working Anytime, Anywhere: The Effects on the World of Work*, Geneva: International Labour Office.

Michelson, W and Lindén, K P (1997) 'Home and telework in Sweden', a paper presented at the Gender and Teleworking Conference, National Resource Centre for Women (NUTEK), Stockholm, Sweden, 14 March.

Microsoft (2021) *2021 Work Trend Index: Annual Report*, Washington, DC: Microsoft.

Miraftab, F (1996) 'Space, gender, and work: home-based workers in Mexico', in Boris, E and Prügl, E (eds) *Homeworkers in Global Perspective: Invisible No More*, London: Routledge.

Mirchandani, K (2000) ' "The best of both worlds" and "cutting my own throat": contradictory images of home-based work', *Qualitative Sociology*, 23(2): 159–182.

Moore, J (2006) 'Homeworking and work-life balance: does it add to quality of life?', *European Review of Applied Psychology*, 56(1): 5–13.

Moore, S (2017) *An Evaluation of UNISON's Ethical Care Charter*, London: University of Greenwich.

Nippert-Eng C (1996) *Home and Work: Negotiating Boundaries Through Everyday Life*, Chicago: University of Chicago Press.

Ojala, S, Nätti, J and Anttila, T (2014) 'Informal overtime at home instead of telework: increase in negative work-family interface', *International Journal of Sociology and Social Policy*, 34(1–2): 69–87.

Pocock, B (2021) 'As boundaries between work and home vanish, employees need a "right to disconnect" ', *The Conversation*, 29 April.

Prospect (2021) *Right to Disconnect: A Guide for Union Activists*, London: Prospect.

Reuschke, D (2019) 'The subjective well-being of homeworkers across life domains', *Economy and Space*, 51(6): 1326–1349.

Royal Society for Public Health (2021) 'Survey reveals the mental and physical health impacts of home working during Covid-19', www.rsph.org.uk/about-us/news/survey-reveals-the-mental-and-physical-health-impacts-of-home-working-during-covid-19.html (accessed 25 July 2021).

Salmi, M (1997) 'Autonomy and time in home-based work', in Heiskanen, T and Rantalaiho, L (eds) *Gendered Practices in Working Life*, London: Palgrave Macmillan.

Scottish Government (2019) *Scottish Business Pledge: Proposal Form*, Glasgow: Scottish Government.

Shamir, B (1992) 'Home: the perfect workplace?', in Zeldeck, S (ed) *Work, Families and Organizations*, San Francisco: Jossey-Bass.

Skountridaki, L, Zschomler, D, Marks, A and Mallett, O (2020) 'Work-life balance for home-based workers amidst a global pandemic', *The Work-Life Bulletin*, 4(2): 16–22.

Spataro, J (2020) 'The future of work – the good, the challenging and the unknown', www.microsoft.com/en-us/microsoft-365/blog/2020/07/08/future-work-good-challenging-unknown/ (accessed 25 July 2021).

Sullivan, C (2000) 'Space and the intersection of work and family in homeworking households', *Community, Work and Family*, 3(2): 185–204.

Taylor, M (2017) *Good Work: The Taylor Review of Modern Working Practices*, London: Department for Business, Energy and Industrial Strategy.

Taylor, P, Scholarios, D and Howcroft, D (2021) *Covid-19 and Working from Home Survey: Preliminary Findings*, Glasgow: University of Strathclyde.

Tietze, S and Musson, G (2002) 'When "work" meets "home": temporal flexibility as lived experience', *Time and Society*, 11(2–3): 315–334.

Vargas-Llave, O, Weber, T and Avogaro, M (2020) *Right to Disconnect in the 27 EU Member States*, Dublin: European Foundation for the Improvement of Living and Working Conditions.

Warren, T (2021) 'Work-time, male-breadwinning and the division of domestic labour: male part-time and full-time workers in unsettled times', *Sociology*, online early view.

Warren, T, Lyonette, C and the UK Women's Budget Group (2021) *Carrying the Work Burden of the Covid-19 Pandemic: Working Class Women in the UK: Final Report*, Nottingham: Nottingham Business School.

Welsh Government (2017) *Code of Practice: Ethical Employment in Supply Chains*, Cardiff: Welsh Government.

Wheatley, D (2012) 'Good to be home? Time-use and satisfaction levels among home-based teleworkers', *New Technology, Work and Employment*, 27(3): 224–241.

Wheatley, D (2016) 'Employee satisfaction and use of flexible working arrangements', *Work, Employment and Society*, 31(4): 567–585.

Wood, S J, Michaelides, G, Inceoglu, I, Hurran, E T, Daniels, K and Niven, K (2021) 'Homeworking, well-being and the COVID-19 pandemic: a diary study', *International Journal of Environmental Research and Public Health*, 18(7575): 1–25.

6 The Future of Remote Working

'Covid has re-shaped our working lives, our economic contributions and our well-being, certainly in the short-term but probably in the longer-term too. Whether this change is for the better is one of the key questions of our time', Andy Haldane, former Chief Economist at the Bank of England, 14 October 2020.

6.1 Introduction

Predicting what might happen in the long term is a dangerous game as we are never quite sure what is around the corner. Back in the 1980s, futurologists were predicting that many of us would be working in 'electronic cottages' by the turn of the millennium. But that never happened. Instead, there was a slow, but steady, detachment of work from place. The change was gradual. Many employees were not trusted to work outside the sight of their bosses. Many may not even have thought that working at home was for them. The 'National Work from Home Day' was set up in response to the resistance of employers and the reluctance of employees to consider it as a viable option. The annual event began in 2006. It continues today and is organised by Work Wise UK, a charity whose mission is to promote smarter ways of working.

However, since the outbreak of coronavirus in March 2020, vast numbers of workers switched – almost overnight – to doing *all* of their paid work at home. Moreover, they had no choice. Society was locked down on a number of occasions, restrictions were imposed on social mixing, and offices were closed. Many workers had not worked at home before and many employers, too, were not used to vast swathes of their staff working outside of their sight. This raises a number of research questions that the chapters in this book have addressed drawing on the best available evidence. What makes homeworking distinctive and worthy of study? What makes today's homeworkers different from those of the past, and how significant has the recent

DOI: 10.4324/9781003247050-6

growth been? What impact has the recent growth of homeworking had on businesses? And how has working at home changed employees' experiences of work? The aim of this final chapter is to examine what the future might hold. Like other chapters in the book, it draws on some of the very best evidence available, but this time the focus is on the long-term implications of 'the great homeworking experiment' (Bloom *et al.*, 2021; Felstead, 2021).

The chapter begins by outlining how attitudes to homeworking and remote working, more generally, have changed following the unprecedented movement of paid work into the home. Employers' reluctance has mellowed and more employees' have experienced the benefits of homeworking. As a result, many employers are more willing to allow their employees to work off-site, completely or for some of the time. By the same token, many employees express the desire to work wholly or partially off-site. The former are remote workers who operate without *any need* to visit their employer's premises; they can work at home or wherever they choose such as the local library, café, or co-working space. The latter are hybrid workers who are also permitted to work in a variety of places, but are *required* to make regular visits back to the office. Some employers and employees, on the other hand, desire a complete return to pre-pandemic ways of working – the daily commute, office hours, and buildings designed for the execution of work. However, with such a prolonged period of working at home, a complete return to pre-pandemic times is unlikely to suit everyone. In this context, the chapter considers the challenges and implications that remote and hybrid working will have for the spatial and temporal organisation of the office and office work. Governments, too, have seen the benefits that reduced travel can have for pollution levels and traffic congestion, but also the challenges that out-of-office working might bring for towns and cities reliant on office workers for business. The chapter closes with a number of research issues that will need to be investigated as the 'new normal' becomes clearer and arrangements – such as remote working and hybrid working – become permanent features of how work is done in the twenty-first century.

6.2 Work Locations of the Future

Evidence from both employees and employers suggests that 'the great homeworking experiment' will become a more entrenched and widely accepted feature of where work is done. However, it is unlikely that work will be exclusively done at home as it was during successive lockdowns imposed by governments across the world. For example, data taken from an online survey of nearly 50,000 workers from across the European Union in April 2021 show that only a minority of employees want to work at home on a daily basis. Nevertheless, the preference to work in this way has risen, and not fallen, over time. It rose from 13% of employees in summer 2020 to 16% in spring 2021. However, around half of employees wished to work on a hybrid basis; that is, combining working at home with working on the employer's premises. Around a third wanted to work at home several times a week and around a fifth wanted to do so several times a month. Only a quarter of employees did not want to work at home at all (Ahrendt *et al.*, 2021).

A similar pattern is repeated in countries around the world. In Canada, for example, those who were new to homeworking in February 2021 were asked about their preferences going forward. The results indicate a strong appetite for working at home; 80% would like to work at least half of the time at home, with 39% wanting to work mostly or exclusively at home. The remaining 20% reported that they would prefer to spend most of their working hours outside of where they live (Mehdi and Morisette, 2021). Evidence from the US, too, reveals a similar pattern. When 2,500 US workers were asked in May 2020 how often they would like to work at home when the pandemic has passed, a quarter said they wanted to become full-time homeworkers. Around a third expressed the desire to combine working at home one to three days a week with their remaining working time spent in the office. In other words, they wished to work on a hybrid basis and, therefore, harness the best of both worlds. This arrangement would lessen the stress and cost of commuting, allow workers to do tasks requiring concentration at home, and free up their office days for face-to-face meetings, socialisation, and collaboration with others. A quarter of respondents did not wish to use the home, even on an occasional basis, as their place of work (Bloom, 2020). This survey has been repeated on multiple occasions since then with similar results (Barrero *et al.*, 2021: Figure 3).

Another indication of the strength of feeling for hybrid working also comes from some of the later waves of the US survey referred to earlier. Respondents were asked how they felt about working at home two or three days a week, the so-called hybrid model. They were given three options: 'positive: I would view it as a benefit or extra pay', 'neutral', and 'negative: I would view it as a cost or a pay cut'. Those giving positive or negative answers were then asked to put a figure on the benefit or cost involved. They were asked to translate the gain or loss in terms of what it would mean for their pay if it were factored in.

The first thing to note is that two-thirds of respondents said they would gain financially from being allowed to work at home two or three days a week. These gains come primarily from reduced commuting costs in terms of time spent travelling and the direct costs involved such as purchasing tickets, maintaining vehicles, and filling them up with petrol. Take commuting time, for example. US workers spent an average of 54 minutes per day commuting to and from work before the pandemic. This is the time that could be saved by working at home (Barrero *et al.*, 2020). Secondly, more than half of workers equated working at home two or three days a week as equivalent to a pay rise of 5% or more. Nearly one in five rated it as equivalent to a pay rise of 15% or more. On the other hand, relatively few thought that hybrid working would be financially costly (Barrero *et al.*, 2021: Figure 4). Employers, therefore, may use the move to hybrid working as a way of putting downward pressure on wages. Big tech companies, such as Google, Microsoft, and Twitter, are contemplating such a move (BBC News, 2021a; *Financial Times*, 17 August 2021). Thirdly, the findings also suggest that the pay-equivalent benefits of hybrid working are greatest for the better educated and the highly paid. Average commuting times, for example, rise with earnings and so does the value placed on working at home. The estimated perk value of hybrid working, therefore, ranges from 1.7% of earnings for those earning less than $50,000 per year to 6.8% of those with earnings of more than $150,000. Similar findings for the value placed on hybrid working and the unequal distribution of these benefits are reported for the UK (Taneja *et al.*, 2021).

Preferences for working at home are also strong in the UK. According to the Understanding Society Covid-19 Study – an online survey of 6,000–7,000 workers – carried out on nine occasions during 2020–2021, the vast majority of those who had worked at home during the pandemic were keen to continue this way of working (Felstead and Reuschke, 2021). Respondents who reported working at home in several of the surveys were asked, 'Once social distancing measures are fully relaxed and workplaces go back to normal, how often would you like to work from home?' Nine out of ten employees who worked at home in June 2020 reported that they would like to continue working at home in some capacity with around one in two employees wanting to work at home often or all of the time. Despite the passage of time, the appetite for homeworking did not decline in later surveys. In fact, nine out of ten homeworkers still wanted to work at home in some capacity when the question was asked in September 2020 and January 2021. However, relatively few wanted to work exclusively at home with three-quarters favouring the hybrid model; that is, working some of the time at home and some of the time on the premises of their employer, typically the office.

Many employers have also responded to the new world. Contrary to their fears, enforced homeworking during the pandemic did not lead to a dip in productivity. In fact, some evidence suggests that working at home actually raised it (see Chapter 4). Employers have improved back-end systems and invested in equipment to support staff working at home. Workers, too, have invested time and money in setting up home offices. As a result, both employers and employees are now better positioned to work at home on a permanent basis or revert back to full-time homeworking if needed.

However, it is commonly agreed that sustaining and improving employee productivity in the long-term will need to be based on some degree of social interaction. Effectively inducting new starters into the organisation is difficult to achieve remotely. Asking for advice and support by email or via Zoom is more awkward than doing so in the kitchen while making a coffee or through a chance encounter when walking around the office. On-the-job learning, too, relies on unintentional visual and aural observation which are built into the typical pre-pandemic open-plan office environment. This drawback is recognised by employers. According to one survey, 70% of businesses said that homeworking during the pandemic had a negative effect on brainstorming activities and 83% said that it reduced the ability of staff to spontaneously share ideas and form new relationships (CBI Economics and University of Leeds, 2021).

In addition, by working outside of the office, employees lose out from many of the social aspects of working with others. This applies especially to those who live on their own and the young. For them, the office is a place to socialise as well as a place to work. After a busy day, they are just as keen as others to close their front door and enjoy some peace and quiet. But solitude while at work and at home is not for them. It is not surprising, then, that young, single employees and couples without children who live in small city centre apartments are among the keenest to be office-based (Bloom, 2021b).

It is for these reasons that many employers, big and small, are rolling out hybrid working arrangements which allow their employees to work more flexibly – some of the time at home (or even elsewhere) and some of the time in the office. Household names – such as Nationwide, Apple, Tui, Google, Facebook, Spotify, NatWest, HSBC, and Deloitte – have announced hybrid working schemes (*Financial Times*, 14 September 2021). Similar plans are also under discussion in many councils, universities, and government departments. However, not all employers are keen on the idea. For example, the boss of Goldman Sachs, David Solomon, dashed bankers' hopes of splitting their time between home and office in February 2021 when he called remote working an 'aberration' that needed to be corrected 'as soon as possible'. In a similar vein, Morgan Stanley's chief executive, James Gorman, told his New York bankers in June 2021 that anyone who felt safe enough to go out to a restaurant should get back to the office.

These individual examples demonstrate that not all employers are keen on making working at home a permanent feature of work. However, the survey evidence suggests that many are. Around a fifth of employers surveyed by the Office for National Statistics (ONS) said that they intended to continue using enhanced levels of homeworking in the future (ONS, 2021). This was in response to the question: 'Does your business intend to use increased homeworking as a permanent business model going forward?' This question was asked in several of the fortnightly Business Insights and Conditions Survey (BICS) carried out by ONS since March 2020.

Other employer surveys also suggest that homeworking is here to stay. For example, the Institute of Directors (IoD) carried out a survey in September 2020 of around 1,000 company directors. It found that nearly three-quarters said they intended to carry on allowing staff to work at home. Furthermore, more than half said their organisation intended to reduce their long-term use of office space and more than one in five reported their usage would be significantly lower (IoD, 2020). Similarly, a survey of 573 businesses carried out by the CBI suggests that homeworking is here to stay. Almost half (47%) predicted that in two or three years' time the majority of their staff would be working in split locations – half of the time in the office and half of the time working off-site. This is up from one in ten (8%) employers in 2019 (CBI, 2020: 4–5). Furthermore, according to a survey of 321 business representatives carried out in May 2021, 93% of UK firms were planning to roll out hybrid working (CBI Economics and University of Leeds, 2021).

Even so, it is important not to exaggerate the extent of the shift. It has been noted, for example, that there are many employers who report that they do *not* intend to use homeworking going forward when questioned by ONS in the survey referred to earlier (Haskel, 2021). So, while 21% of firms say yes they intend to use more homeworking in the future, 48% say no they do not. The percentage of saying no vastly outweighs the percentage of saying yes across all sectors. There are, however, a few exceptions: in information and communication, the proportion saying yes exceeds the proportion saying no by 27 percentage points; in the professional and scientific sector, where the gap is 12 percentage points; and in education, where the proportion saying yes is 6 percentage points greater than the proportion saying no. It should also be noted that the survey does not include the finance and insurance sector, which has been a heavy user of homeworking during the pandemic and might be expected to continue operating in this way in the future (Haskel, 2021: Figure 6).

One should also be aware that homeworking is likely to be on part-time not full-time basis and so hours spent working at home are likely to be lower. A monthly survey of around 9,400 businesses in the UK carried out by the Bank of England, the University of Nottingham, and Stanford University – known as the Decision Maker Survey – found that employers in April 2021 expected 38% of their workforce to be working off-site in 2022.

However, in terms of hours, this is expected to account for 21% of working time as a result of workers opting to work less than five days a week at home. Most employers were expecting hybrid workers to work two or three days a week at home (Decision Maker Panel, 2021)

Analysis of job adverts also suggests heightened interest in remote, hybrid, and homeworking arrangements. When lockdown restrictions began in March 2020, the total number of UK online job adverts fell and did not return to pre-pandemic average levels until the end of April 2021. However, online job adverts including terms related to 'homeworking' – such as remote working, hybrid working, and working from home – reached pre-pandemic average levels by July 2020. By May 2021, such adverts were being posted at 307% of their February 2020 average level (Smith, 2021; Casey, 2021). Recruitment agencies, too, have reported a rapid rise in vacancies advertised as remote working opportunities. According to Reed – the recruitment agency for professionals – such vacancies accounted for 1% of job adverts before the pandemic, but by 2021 this proportion had risen to 5% (BBC News, 2021b). Once again, this suggests that the location of work is becoming more fluid and is increasingly making its way into job adverts designed to attract candidates who prefer to work off-site for at least some of the time.

6.3 Offices of the Future

Even before the pandemic offices were changing. The most significant of these changes was the growth of open-plan office design in the 1960s and 1970s (Laing, 1997; Duffy, 1992). This facilitated greater visibility by managers of their staff and made employees more visible to their colleagues. However, stripping down office walls did not eliminate the idea of personal space; that is, a chair, desk, and personal computer allocated to an individual worker for their own use. Indeed, workers often responded to open-plan office environments by attempting to make themselves less visible as walls and partitions were removed. For example, by using equipment to recreate dividing walls, thereby marking out symbolic boundaries around their personal office space (Goffman, 1959, 1971).

A further shift came in the 1990s with the sharing of space and equipment. Occupancy surveys showed that space and equipment set aside for single-person use – referred to as personal offices – were rarely fully occupied. Workers were away from their desks when visiting clients, consulting colleagues, attending meetings, looking up information, on holiday, and off sick. Some surveys even suggested that workstations and offices might go unoccupied for as much as two-thirds of a typical working week (Turner and Myerson, 1998: 70; Zelinsky, 1997: 48–56). When weekends and holidays were factored in, the cost of unused space rose even further (Nathan and Doyle, 2002). Attention, therefore, turned to more efficient use of office space and equipment. Hence, the growing use of hot desks – workstations not 'owned' by any one individual, but available to all on a first-come-first-served basis – and the use of office equipment, such as printers, to which everyone had access. This has been referred to as the 'collective office' since space is no longer allocated on an individual basis, but is shared with others (Felstead *et al.*, 2005).

Any sustained change in the location of work – through remote and hybrid working arrangements – will mean that *more* employees spend *more* time away from the office, thereby further reducing the need for office space. Employers may therefore seek smaller and more dispersed offices. This will enable employers to cater more efficiently for the needs of a workforce that visits the office more infrequently as well as providing employers with an opportunity to lower their estate costs.

However, using smaller offices for a hybrid workforce brings challenges. One concern is that given the choice, most employees will choose to work at home on Mondays and Fridays. According to one UK survey, only 36% of employees would choose to come into the office on Friday compared to 82% on Wednesday (Bloom *et al.*, 2021). If employers provide all employees with a desk so they can work in the office on Wednesdays, most of these desks would be unoccupied on the favoured working at home days of Mondays and Fridays. This would thwart any attempt to move to smaller premises. To complicate the picture, those wishing to work away from the office are likely to be different from those who are content to go back to the office full-time. Those keenest on time away from the office tend to be working mothers. Therefore, allowing employees to choose whether to come into the office or not is likely to reduce the diversity of the office-based workforce. Furthermore, we know from other research (see Chapter 5) that those 'out of sight' are more likely to be passed over for promotion than those seen by managers on daily basis. Single men who choose to go to the office five days a week are more likely to get promoted, while working mothers who choose to work at home are less likely to move up the career ladder.

One solution to both of these problems is to specify the days of the week on which all team members must be on site. If a skeleton on-site presence is required every day of the week, employees need to be rostered to come in on those days. On the other days of the week, employees should be allowed to work off-site. However, coordination across the organisation is required to ensure that the building is not empty on some days and overcrowded on others. Teams that often work together also need to liaise with one another to make sure that they have at least two days of overlap when they are both in the office. New recruits, too, need special attention. One suggestion is that they come into the office an extra day a week for the first year in order to get to know their colleagues and 'learn the ropes' (Bloom, 2021a).

All of this requires coordination, planning, and leadership. This is additional work that will need to be done for hybrid working to operate successfully. Research suggests that these additional duties – like celebrating colleagues' birthdays, organising office social events, and mentoring junior members of staff – tend to fall on the shoulders of women. For example, experimental studies of who does these kinds of 'office chores' suggest that women are more likely to volunteer to do them or else feel under pressure to do so (Babcock *et al.*, 2017). While facilitating the move to hybrid working, volunteering to coordinate who will be in the office and when is an additional task that is unlikely to carry much recognition. Employers will, therefore, need to consider valuing and recognising these additional tasks so that hybrid working operates successfully.

6.4 Society of the Future

Early advocates of homeworking emphasised its environmental benefits by coining the term 'telecommuting'. This referred to using technology to work at or near home, thereby minimising the need to travel to and from a place of work (Nilles, 1991). However, apart from during occasional fuel shortages – such as the tanker driver dispute of 2000 when petrol supplies were in short supply for several weeks – greater use of homeworking as a way of minimising travel was not really considered a viable policy option. The situation has changed markedly since then.

Heightened awareness of the environment damage caused by the burning of fossil fuels – with the UK Government declaring a climate emergency in 2019 – and the enforced use of homeworking during the pandemic has led to many organisations considering how they can minimise their carbon footprint. The UK is legally committed by the *Climate Change Act 2008* to reduce carbon emissions by 80% relative to their 1990 levels by 2050. However, some city and local councils have set a more ambitious target. They aim to become carbon neutral by 2030 by using renewable energy supplies, building more energy-efficient housing and introducing a host of other measures, including the promotion of remote and hybrid working. Private employers, too, are thinking along the same lines with moves towards becoming carbon neutral being made by Amazon, Microsoft, Sky, Google, and Marks & Spencer.

One of the biggest and most noticeable effects of locking society down and limiting mobility was the drop in traffic. Roads became quieter and roadside pollution levels fell. But the scale of the environment impact is debatable. For example, the decline in nitrogen dioxide was lower than the decline in traffic levels would suggest. This is because the number of heavily emitting vehicles on roads, such as diesel-powered freight trucks, fell only slightly compared to commuter traffic. Also although fewer people were going to the office, many were using cars for local journeys when previously they would have used less polluting buses or trains.

In addition, using the home as a place to work meant that the heating was on for longer. To make matters worse, homes tend to be heated using gas-burning boilers which are more polluting than electric heating systems commonly used in offices (Monks, 2020; Shi and Bloss, 2021). Looking to the future, if office workers spend more of their time working from poorly insulated houses, and businesses continue to heat, cool, and light large offices which are left half-empty most of the time, but available for when hybrid workers have their 'office days', then the net effect may be that carbon emissions rise. All of this suggests that remote and hybrid working have positive and negative impacts on the environment. It cannot, therefore, be assumed that these ways of working will be good for the environment since they may lower emissions in some cases, but shift them around and even increase them in others. Existing research suggests that the impact of remote working on energy use is complicated (Hook *et al.*, 2020). Furthermore, given the uncertainties about the precise pattern of working in the future, it is difficult to predict - at the moment - the net effect that greater use of the home as a place of work will have on carbon emissions.

One possible break on the home as a place of work in the future is the strength of digital infrastructure, notably the existence of an internet connection and one which is quick enough to carry out video calls and/or exchange documents and data. Even today, not all parts of the UK even have an internet connection and when they do it may be too slow to carry out essential everyday tasks. This does not just apply to rural parts of the UK – such as in the foothills of the Preseli mountains in rural Wales or the national park in Dartmoor – but to major towns and cities. For example, while broadband speeds are generally faster in urban areas compared with rural ones, this is often the result of strong investment in the suburbs. As a result, internet speeds can be very poor in the centre of cities such as London, Manchester, Liverpool, and Birmingham (*Financial Times*, 17 July 2018).

The housing market will also be affected by any long-term shift towards remote and hybrid working. The prospect of spending more time working at home has already prompted the start of a 'race for space'. The looser the physical ties to the office become, the more likely it is that workers will live further away from the office. House prices reflected this tendency during the pandemic. They rose much faster outside central London than in the surrounding boroughs or even further afield (Hunter, 2021). Similarly, house prices on the outskirts of major cities rose more strongly than in the cities they surround (*Financial Times*, 28–29 August 2021). If remote and hybrid working become permanent features of the way we work, this shift is likely to continue; more people will move out of cities to areas with a good internet connection and into houses with more space.

One of the most visible signs of the pandemic was the negative and dramatic effect it had on city centres and the high street. This was frequently illustrated in news bulletins with photographs of deserted city centres and empty high streets with bars, restaurants, and shops boarded up. Even when lockdown restrictions were eased and hospitality and retail were permitted to reopen, footfall did not bounce back to its pre-lockdown level. As outlined earlier, many employees have continued to work at home and do not want to come into the office as frequently as they did before, even when social distancing is a thing of the past. Many of these offices are located in city centres which bring in high-value customers for businesses, such as bars, restaurants, and shops.

However, the spending power of office workers will not disappear, but will shift towards similar businesses nearer to where they live as opposed to the city centres where they used to work. So, instead of picking up a coffee on the way to the office, popping out to have a haircut in their lunch hour or doing a spot of shopping after work, their demands for such services will be met by businesses operating in the local neighbourhood and not in the city centre. In other words, some of the purchasing power of office workers who spend more time working at home will shift from city centres to local neighbourhoods (Shone, 2020; Ramuni, 2020).

Data taken from the Annual Survey of Hours and Earnings (ASHE) have been used to estimate the scale of these shifts in spending. For this survey, employers are asked a limited number of questions about the jobs of specified members of staff. These staff form part of a 1% sample of employee jobs randomly drawn from HM Revenue and Customs Pay as You Earn (PAYE) records. In addition to detailed occupation and earnings information, the survey also collects geographic data on where job holders work and where they live. The survey is carried out by ONS every April (Smith, 2020).

By adding together ASHE data taken from several years, it is possible to analyse the data at a much finer geographical level than would be possible by focusing on one year's worth of data. These include areas that contain a population of between 5,000 and 15,000 people. There are around 7,000 such geographical areas in mainland Britain. Technically speaking, these are known as Middle Layer Super Output Areas (MSOA) in Wales and England, and Intermediate Zones (IZ) in Scotland. By adding together ASHE data of 2017, 2018, and 2019, researchers have examined what effect a long-term shift to remote working might have on spending patterns in these small geographical areas (De Fraja *et al.*, 2021).

The results are threefold. First, before the pandemic most people did not work and live in the same geographical area, instead they travelled to and from work. Only 11% of employees worked and lived in the same MSOA and in over 97% of MSOAs more than 60% of residents moved out of the area for work (i.e. they commuted). Inevitably, the proportion of commuters decreases the larger the geographical area; individuals in larger areas have travel longer distances to move beyond their home territories and become designated as 'commuters'. But even at the local authority level (of which there are around 400 in Britain) commuting across boundaries before the pandemic was strong. Almost half of residents commuted to a different local authority to do their work.

Secondly, the potential to work remotely varies geographically (cf. Chapter 3). It is particularly high in areas which rely on commuters such as central London and large cities such as Newcastle and Nottingham. For example, three-quarters of employees in the City of London and half of those in Westminster are estimated to have the potential to work at home (De Fraja *et al.*, 2021: Table 1). On the other hand, the suburbs and outer reaches of large cities have the most to gain if the working at home becomes the norm. By definition, these employees will stay closer to their place of residence. Thirdly, therefore, they are more likely to buy a sandwich, get their hair cut or do some shopping locally. This will result in a supply and demand mismatch since local high streets are not as well developed as they are in large cities. For example, the evidence shows that over half of service employment – restaurant and bar staff, shop workers, and hairdressers – are employed in areas which predicted to experience a net reduction in commuting, but these locations account for just 28% of all areas. Businesses may, therefore, need to relocate to where the demand for their services reappears.

Evidence also suggests that some homeworkers find it difficult to reconcile home and work life, feel unsupported and isolated, and have difficulty switching off (cf. Chapter 5). Low-cost community hubs may mitigate some of these problems by providing workers with the opportunity to work in a 'third space' that is neither home nor office. Experiments are currently underway in parts of the UK to estimate the scale of the demand for spaces where employees can rent a desk and congregate with others while carrying out their own work (Gandini, 2015; Reuschke *et al.*, 2021a, 2021b). This may also provide an opportunity to repurpose government buildings, office blocks, and other locations which are no longer fully occupied, but could be used by workers who happen to live close by or wish to use a third space.

Governments, too, are considering the implications of the longer term shift towards remote and hybrid working. The UK Government, for example, reconvened the Flexible Working Task Force in February 2021. It is jointly chaired by a government minister from the Department for Business, Energy and Industrial Strategy (BEIS) and the chief executive of the Chartered Institute of Personnel and Development (CIPD). Its membership draws from business lobby organisations, professional bodies, unions, and charities. The group's remit is to develop policies and practices to support new ways of working. This includes: making it easier for employees to work at home; helping employees to disconnect from work; and considering whether more could be done to promote 'ad hoc' or 'non-contractual' working at home arrangements. The group is due to sit for 18 months.

Although the Welsh Government (and the other devolved governments) do not have legislative powers over matters relating to employment, it has gone a step further by stating that its long-term ambition is 'to see around 30% of Welsh workers working from home or near to home' even in the absence of the need for social distancing. This now forms part of its five-year programme for the government (Welsh Government, 2020, 2021). The Irish Government has made a similar commitment, but it has set a lower target of 20%. However, this target only applies to the public sector (Government of Ireland, 2021). Other governments – such as the Japanese, Portuguese, and Finnish – signalled their desire to promote homeworking among their own staff long before the pandemic began (Messenger *et al.*, 2017: 45–46).

6.5 Conclusion: Future Research

To prevent the spread of coronavirus there was a sudden and dramatic shift in the location of work. Almost overnight many workers had to convert their bedrooms into offices, their living room tables into desks, and their kitchens into places of work. Employers, too, have had to manage staff remotely, many for the first time. Not surprisingly, interest in how employees and employers have coped with this revolution in working practices has exploded. The overall aim of this book is to sketch out the issues this raises along with the historical debates which have preceded this dramatic turn of events. It is not the final word on the subject, far from it.

The book ends with an outline of some of the future-orientated research questions which will need to be addressed.

- How extensive will homeworking, remote working, and hybrid working be in the future?
- What type of employees and employers will make greatest use of these ways of working? Will some lose out and others gain, and will this lessen or increase patterns of inequality?

- To what extent, and in what ways, will employees and employers revert to previous practices?
- How will the downsides of off-site working to employees – the dangers of overworking, the disruption to work–life balance, the drawbacks of becoming an outsider, and the feeling of isolation – be tackled by employers, trade unions, and government?
- What type of employees are most at risk and how can employers mitigate these effects?
- What will the impact of more off-site working have on job quality, such as uncertainties about the job itself and its security, involvement in decision-making, and prospects for a pay increase?
- What steps will employers take to mitigate the ill effects of remote and hybrid working, such as incidental learning, team building, and onboarding new staff which rely on face-to-face contact?
- What impact will an increase in homeworking, remote working, and/or hybrid working have for the environment, employee productivity, and who does what in the home?
- What impact will the relocation of work have on the size and layout of the offices that remain, their location, and the way office work is managed?
- How will city centres and local high streets cope with a sustained shift of work into the home and other non-office spaces? What impact will the shift have on the housing market and the design of homes?

No doubt future conference presentations, articles, and even books will tackle some of these issues as well as a host of others. Research projects – student dissertations, commissioned reports, and academic studies – will multiply. This will require analysis of official and unofficial data sets, the development of new survey questions, and the collection of additional information via new surveys, case studies, and interviews. This will provide a sound basis on which to assess the impact of the changing location of work on businesses, employees, and the towns and cities in which we live and work. Only then can we properly respond to the quotation cited at the beginning of this chapter and evaluate whether any of the sustained changes to the location of work have made the world better or worse. It is hoped that this book has provided some of the groundwork on which this judgement can eventually be made.

References

Ahrendt, D, Mascherini, M, Nivakoski, S and Sándor, E (2021) *Living, Working and COVID-19 (Update April 2021)*, Dublin: European Foundation for the Improvement of Living and Working Conditions.

Babcock, L, Recalde, M P, Vesterlund, L and Weingart, L (2017) 'Gender differences in accepting and receiving requests for tasks with low promotability', *American Economic Review*, 107(3): 714–747.

Barrero, J M, Bloom, N and Davis, S J (2020) *60 Million Fewer Commuting Hours Per Day: How Americans Use Time Saved by Working from Home*, Becker Friedman Institute Working Paper, No. 132, Chicago: Becker Friedman Institute.

Barrero, J M, Bloom, N and Davis, S J (2021) *Why Working from Home Will Stick*, NBER Working Paper Series, Working Paper, No. 28731, Cambridge, MA: National Bureau of Economic Research.

BBC (2021a) 'Google may cut pay of staff who work from home', 12 August, www.bbc.co.uk/news/business-58171716 (accessed 19 August 2021).

BBC (2021b) 'Working from home job adverts rise, by Leanna Bryne and BBC Staff', 11 August, www.bbc.co.uk/news/business-58160245 (accessed 19 August 2021).

Bloom, N (2020) *How Working from Home Works Out*, Stanford Institute for Economic Policy Research (SIEPR) Policy Brief, Stanford: SIEPR, June.

Bloom, N (2021a) 'Don't let employees pick their WFH days', *Harvard Business Review Magazine*, 25 May.

Bloom, N (2021b) *Hybrid Is the Future of Work*, Stanford Institute for Economic Policy Research (SIEPR) Policy Brief, Stanford: SIEPR, June.

Bloom, N, Mizen, P and Taneja, S (2021) 'Returning to the office will be hard', *VoxEU*, 15 June, https://voxeu.org/article/returning-office-will-be-hard (accessed 12 August 2021).

Casey, A (2021) *Business and Individual Attitudes Towards the Future of Homeworking, UK: April to May 2021*, Newport: Office for National Statistics.

CBI (2020) *No Turning Back*, London: Confederation of British Industry.

CBI Economics and University of Leeds (2021) *The Revolution of Work: A Survey on the World of Work Post-COVID-19*, London: Confederation of Business Industry.

Decision Maker Panel (2021) 'Aggregate results tables – monthly data', July (Excel), https://decisionmakerpanel.co.uk/data/ (accessed 12 August 2021).

De Fraja, G, Matheson, J and Rockey, J (2021) 'Zoomshock: the geography and local labour market consequences of working from home', *Covid Economics*, 64: 1–41.

Duffy, F (1992) *The Changing Workplace*, London: Phaidon Press.

Felstead, A (2021) *Outlining the Contours of the "Great Homeworking Experiment" and Its Implications for Wales*, Senedd Economy, Infrastructure and Skills Committee Commissioned Report, Cardiff: Senedd Cymru.

Felstead, A, Jewson, N and Walters, S (2005) *Changing Places of Work*, Basingstoke: Palgrave Macmillan.

Felstead, A and Reuschke, D (2021) 'A flash in the pan or a permanent change? The growth of homeworking during the pandemic and its effect on employee productivity in the UK', *Information Technology and People*, online first.

Financial Times (2018) 'Broadband speed map reveals Britain's new digital divide, by A Smith, N Fildes, D Blood, M Harlow, C Nevitt, and A Rinisland', *Financial Times*, 17 July.

Financial Times (2021) 'Cutting pay for remote workers is a risky move, by S O'Connor', *Financial Times*, 17 August.

Financial Times (2021) 'The flexibility factor: who is going back to the office?, by A Hill', *Financial Times*, 14 September.

Financial Times (2021) 'Rise in homeworking drives house price boom outside cities, by V Romei', *Financial Times*, 28–29 August.

Gandini, A (2015) 'The rise of coworking spaces: a literature review', *Ephemera*, 15(1): 193–205.

Goffman, E (1959) *The Presentation of Self in Everyday Life*, London: Penguin.

Goffman, E (1971) *Relations in Public: Microstudies of the Public Order*, London: Penguin.

Government of Ireland (2021) *Making Remote Work: National Remote Work Strategy*, Dublin: Department of Enterprise, Trade and Industry.

Haskel, J (2021) 'What is the future of working from home?', *Economic Observatory*, April, www.economicsobservatory.com/what-is-the-future-of-working-from-home (accessed 11 August 2021).

Hook, A, Court, V, Sovocool, B K and Sorrell, S (2020) 'A systematic review of the energy and climate impacts of teleworking', *Environmental Research Letters*, 15: 1–30.

Hunter, P (2021) *Planning for the Recovery and the Shift Towards Homeworking: Implications for Poverty in Outer London*, London: The Smith Institute.

IoD (2020) 'Home-working here to stay, new IoD figures suggest', *IoD Press Release*, 5 October.

Laing, A (1997) 'New patterns of work: the design of the office', in Worthington, J (ed) *Reinventing the Workplace*, Oxford: Architectural Press.

Mehdi, T and Morisette, R (2021) *Working from Home: Productivity and Preferences*, Ottawa: Statistics Canada.

Messenger, J, Vargas-Llave, O, Gschwind, L, Boehmer, S, Vermeylen, G and Wilkens, M (2017) *Working Anytime, Anywhere: The Effects on the World of Work*, Geneva: International Labour Office.

Monks, P (2020) 'Coronavirus: lockdown's effect on air pollution provides a rare glimpse of low-carbon future', *The Conversation*, 15 April.

Nathan, M and Doyle, J (2002) *The State of the Office: The Politics and Geography of Working Space*, London: Industrial Society.

Nilles, J M (1991) 'Telecommuting and urban sprawl: mitigator or inciter?', *Transportation*, 18(4): 411–432.

ONS (2021) *BICS: Wave 14 to Wave 24 Working from Home Questions Weighted by Employment*, Newport: Office for National Statistics, www.ons.gov.uk/businessindustryandtrade/business/businessservices/adhocs/13124bicswave14towave24workingfromhomequestionsweightedbyemployment (accessed 12 August 2021).

Ramuni, L (2020) 'Why working from home hurts the high street', *Centre for Cities Blog Post*, 1 July, www.centreforcities.org/blog/why-working-from-home-hurts-the-high-street/ (accessed 15 August 2021).

Reuschke, D, Clifton, N and Fisher, M (2021a) 'Coworking in homes – mitigating the tensions of the freelance economy', *Geoforum*, 119: 122–132.

Reuschke, D, Clifton, N and Long, J (2021b) *Remote Working – Spatial Implications in Wales*, Senedd Economy, Infrastructure and Skills Committee Commissioned Report, Cardiff: Senedd Cymru.

Shi, Z and Bloss, W (2021) 'First lockdown's effect on air pollution was overstated, our study reveals', *The Conversation*, 13 January.

Shone, G (2020) *Shifting Working Patterns: How WFH Could Be the High Street's Saviour*, London: Radius Data Exchange.

Smith, R (2020) *Employee Earnings in the UK: 2020*, Newport: Office for National Statistics.

Smith, R (2021) *Using Adzuna Data to Derive an Indicator to Derive Weekly Vacancies: Experimental Statistics*, Newport: Office for National Statistics.

Taneja, S, Mizen, P and Bloom, N (2021) 'Working from home is revolutionising the UK labour market', *VoxEu*, 15 March, https://voxeu.org/article/working-home-revolutionising-uk-labour-market (accessed 11 August 2021).

Turner, G and Myerson, J (1998) *New Workspace, New Culture*, London: Gower.

Welsh Government (2020) *Aim for 30% of the Welsh Workforce to Work Remotely*, Welsh Government Press Release, Cardiff: Welsh Government, 13 September.

Welsh Government (2021) *Programme for Government*, Cardiff: Welsh Government.

Zelinsky, M (1997) *New Workplaces for New Workstyles*, New York: McGraw-Hill.

Index

Note: Page numbers in *italics* indicate a figure and page numbers in **bold** indicate a table on the corresponding page.

For Product Safety Concerns and Information please contact our EU
representative GPSR@taylorandfrancis.com Taylor & Francis Verlag GmbH,
Kaufingerstraße 24, 80331 München, Germany

Printed and bound by CPI Group (UK) Ltd, Croydon, CR0 4YY

01/05/2025

01858334-0001